God's Church for God's World

God's Church for God's World

A PRACTICAL APPROACH TO PARTNERSHIP IN MISSION

Edited by Robert S. Heaney,
John Kafwanka K, and Hilda Kabia

CHURCH
PUBLISHING
INCORPORATED

Church Publishing
19 East 34th Street
New York, NY 10016
www.churchpublishing.org

Cover design by Jennifer Kopec, 2Pug Design
Typeset by PerfecType Design, Nashville, Tennessee

Library of Congress Cataloging-in-Publication Data
Names: Lambeth Conference (2020 : University of Kent at Canterbury) |
   Heaney, Robert Stewart, 1972- editor. | Kafwanka, John, editor. | Kabia,
   Hilda, editor.
Title: God's church for God's world : a practical approach to partnership
   in mission / edited by Robert S. Heaney, John Kafwanka & Hilda Kabia.
Identifiers: LCCN 2019045499 (print) | LCCN 2019045500 (ebook) | ISBN
   9781640650527 (paperback) | ISBN 9781640650534 (ebook)
Subjects: LCSH: Missions--Congresses. | Anglican
   Communion--Doctrines--Congresses.
Classification: LCC BV2020 .L36 2020 (print) | LCC BV2020 (ebook) | DDC
   266/.3--dc23
LC record available at https://lccn.loc.gov/2019045499
LC ebook record available at https://lccn.loc.gov/2019045500

Contents

Acknowledgments

It is no small task to bring together a diverse range of voices from throughout the Communion and beyond. The editors are, therefore, grateful to a number of people who have made this possible. Research assistants in Virginia Theological Seminary's Center for Anglican Communion Studies—Jean-Pierre Seguin, Valerie Mayo, and Jean Cotting—exhibited care and commitment in communication, proofreading, locating sources, and "other tasks assigned"! The center's staff, Hartley Wensing and Molly O'Brien, in many and real ways ground the vision of "promoting and practicing community for the Communion." The completion of this book is further testament to their hope in God's future.

Leaders in the Communion and staff at the Anglican Communion Office have been thoughtful and helpful partners in this project. Without their suggestions and advice, this resource would be the poorer. It was a delight to work with Nancy Bryan and Milton Brasher-Cunningham at Church Publishing, New York. Their encouragement, vision, and professionalism have made this beautiful resource a reality.

We also wish to pay tribute to our authors. Each one of them leads busy lives and has busy and demanding roles in their communities. We are honored that, even amidst it all, they were prepared to offer such rich and reflective work on the nature and call of God's people in God's world. Archbishop Justin Welby has written a fitting foreword to the collection and we are deeply grateful to him.

Robert is thankful for the leadership and collegiality that Virginia Theological Seminary provides, the collegiality of the Lambeth Conference

Design Group, and the many Anglicans from throughout the world he has the privilege of meeting and working with. He gives thanks to God for the grace and blessing of his wife, Dr. Sharon E. Heaney, and son, Sam.

John wishes to recognize the encouragement and support of the Most Revd Dr. Josiah Idowu-Fearon, secretary general of the Anglican Communion, and all the staff at the Anglican Communion Office. He is especially thankful to his wife, Martha, and children, Mwila and Limbani, for their patience, endurance, and love. Finally, John wishes to acknowledge the support of many leaders, lay and ordained, throughout the Anglican Communion who have enriched his understanding and appreciation of mutuality in partnerships and in God's unconditional love for humanity.

Hilda gives thanks to God for his love and for keeping the authors and editors healthy during the fieldwork and composition of this book. Her sincere gratitude is extended to her fellow editors, Robert and John, for their patience, constructive thoughts, and valuable comments while editing this book.

Foreword

The first letter of Peter is a lesser-known treasure in the New Testament. It is a letter that explores the depth of what it means to be Church, to be a Christian, in a hostile world. It is a letter about the identity of the people of God, as holy and dearly loved. The Church is told to be holy, as the Lord our God is holy. The Church is to look like the face of God upon the earth, to radiate His holiness outward. This is why I chose 1 Peter for us to reflect on at the 2020 Lambeth Conference. It is a text that calls us back to the core of who we are before God; it is a text that reminds us of how precious the Church is, how precious every brother and sister is, however much we may disagree with them. It is a letter that bears both immense comfort and immense challenge, a letter which, at its core, is all about keeping our eyes fixed on Jesus as we wrestle with our place in the world, our calling as disciples, our engagement with all the big questions of our time.

At the heart of 1 Peter are the questions, "What is your purpose as a disciple of Jesus Christ? What does it mean to live as one who has not only accepted but lives by the word of God?" The text does not give easy answers, but instead invites us to walk the way of Christ. The letter looks to the heart of each disciple, to the heart of the Church, and invites them to consistently look outward and consider their engagement with the wider world. The purpose of discipleship is to transform the world by living as though God's kingdom of heaven already reigns over all the earth. It is for the Church to be deeply involved in our world, to educate children, to treat the sick, and to provide refuge for the poor in our communities.

The Church has another identity: our identity as a family. We do not get to choose each other—and whether we argue or not, nothing will change the

fact that we will all still be family at the end of the day. A key part in that famil-
ial identity is our diversity. How do we relate to those who are different from
us? We start and end with our common bond that is stronger than anything
else: Jesus Christ. We listen to the lived experiences of our friends in Christ; we
stand with them in their struggles and rejoice in their triumphs. We return to
His table, no matter how far we may have wandered, and welcome all others
to sit beside us, to be nourished by Him and His unconditional love for us.

When we return to Christ's table, it is a chance for us to look upon each
other as God looks at us. We can take peace and comfort from the fact that
God understands division, persecution, oppression, and violence intimately.
He is the Christ who was crucified, mocked, and jeered. And yet he is still the
Christ who died for our sakes, even when we had rejected him. How do we
follow His example—would we be willing to lay down our life for those with
whom we argue bitterly?

As we listen, walk, and witness with each other in the pages of this book,
so I hope we meet with God afresh. These chapters, written to and for people
with a range of different backgrounds and experiences, illustrate perfectly
how collaboration and partnership among different cultures and thinking can
enhance our understanding of the gospel, build a better and more compre-
hensive picture of God's Church, and help us to realize God's great mission.
The Church does not just look like those who think similarly, who agree on
everything, who come from the same place and have the same experiences—it
should look like every single one of us. It should look like God Himself.

It is my hope that readers of this wonderful book might be inspired and
reenergized in their personal spiritual lives, in their communities, and in the
wider Church. I hope that we might all seek to nurture new life and new beginnings, to celebrate the many remarkable things the Church is doing around
the world, to stand in solidarity with our brothers and sisters, to witness to our
salvation through Jesus Christ, and to be inspired to follow Christ in all places,
at all times, so that we can see the gospel at work in every aspect of our world.

Justin Welby
Archbishop of Canterbury

Introduction

Robert S. Heaney, John Kafwanka K, and Hilda Kabia

The Lambeth Conference of 2020 chose as its theme "God's Church for God's World." Such a title describes the work of the Church, but it also describes the call and nature of the Church. The Church is created by God and it is called to witness to God's love in the world. Anglicans take this seriously. We believe that this Church is called by God into neighborhoods and nations to proclaim and embody the good news of God's love to all people. That is to say, the Church exists as a community of disciples sent out into the world by the risen Christ. Amidst the diversity and challenges of the world and the solidarities and opportunities that present themselves to humanity—the Church, as the community of the resurrected one, seeks signs of new life, seeks to nurture new life, and seeks to be a sign of new life in God's world. That is the focus of this book. In ten chapters, you will be invited to discern new life in your context and to act for new life in your community. Each chapter is cowritten by two authors from distinct cultural and theological perspectives. Fifteen nations or nationalities from across the world are represented. As well as Anglican voices in this volume, you will also hear from Lutheran, Uniting Reformed, Jewish, and Muslim authors.

The subtitle to this book is as important as the main title. This is a book that is *practical*. By that we mean at least three things. First, the authors in this book are not only theologians, they are also practitioners. They draw on significant experience across a range of disciplines and in a range of contexts. Second, the book is written as an invitation for readers to consider their own context and experience. Each chapter invites you to reflect on scripture, to listen to voices from beyond your context, and to pray asking God's Spirit to deepen your faith and commitment to renewed practice. Third, with questions for discussion, Bible study, and liturgy, this book is designed not only for individual reflection but also as a practical resource for church groups and community groups in ongoing programs of formation. In *God's Church for God's World,* churches, vestries, organizations, dioceses, and provinces will be encouraged to compare their understandings and practices with those from other settings. You will be encouraged to revisit and renew priorities and ministries as your faith community seeks to take heed of and participate in the one mission of the one God.

In chapter one, Robert S. Heaney and John Kafwanka K remind us that mission is inextricably linked to the human response to God's grace-filled mission in creation and in re-creation. Mission, in other words, is part of Christian formation. Given that Anglicans are presently in a season of "Intentional Discipleship and Disciple-Making," this approach will remain important.[1] In reflection on Ephesians chapter one, stories from around the world, and principles for good partnership, they invite consideration of discipleship in the mission of God.

Alan Yarborough and Marie Carmel Chery, in chapter two, remind us that Christian witness does not only mean talking. It also means listening. Indeed, when sisters and brothers do not listen well, unhealthy models of partnership emerge. This they illustrate with stories from Haiti and in reflections on 1 Peter 2. In reading this text they recall the transformative revelation that we are called by God. The divine calling is to know more profoundly the eternal love of God and to share it with others. Yarborough and Chery illustrate that such sharing begins in close listening.

In chapter three, Sarah Hills and Deon Snyman recognize that despite a common call to mission and learning from one another, deep divisions can

---

1. See Resolution 16.01 from the Anglican Consultative Council (2016), accessed August 20, 2019, https://www.anglicancommunion.org/structures/instruments-of -communion/acc/acc-16/resolutions.aspx#s1.

develop. Any fellowship, whether local or global, will experience disagreement. Rather than see this as a problem, they call us toward disagreeing well. Beginning on the road to Emmaus (Luke 24), we learn from the risen Jesus. Jesus, in modeling good disagreement, brought his friends into deeper realization of God's grace. Hills and Snyman, reflecting the realities of a broken world today, provide counterexamples of bad disagreement from Zimbabwe and South Africa. They conclude with spiritual and practical exercises to help move communities toward disagreeing well.

Gloria Mapangdol and Paulo Ueti, in chapter four, argue for the centrality of hospitality in understandings and practices of mission. While drawing from a variety of biblical sources, they choose to focus on the writing of Luke. In this literature there is a strong emphasis on the eternal unconditional love of God over and against the experiences and expectations of humans and human communities throughout the ages. Hospitality expresses the radical love of God. This is a message particularly welcomed by the marginalized, and the authors illustrate how it has informed ministries and priorities in Brazil and the Philippines.

Chapter five deals with the concept and practice of communion as "disciplined sharing." Janice Price and John Kapya Kaoma, in light of the "Jerusalem collection" (2 Cor. 8–9), define disciplined sharing as practical ministry within established relationships and structures. *Ubuntu* comes close to this biblical understanding of sharing as it celebrates the connectedness of all people to local community and to the human family. Price and Kaoma illustrate disciplined sharing with stories from Sierra Leone, Zambia, and England, arguing for the life-giving potential of companion links in the Anglican Communion.

Mutuality as life-giving discipleship is explored by Cornelia Eaton and James Stambaugh in chapter six. Reflecting on Philippians 2 and the *Diné* way of life called *hozhó,* Eaton and Stambaugh invite us into a rich reflection on human interconnectedness and Christian mutuality. They call for renewed practices of prayer, training that opens our eyes to the presence of the creator in creation, table fellowship, listening, storytelling, and partnership in mission.

In chapter seven, Anne Burghardt and John Gibaut provide an ecumenical reading of the New Testament vision of *koinonia* (communion). From that point of departure, they explain how a commitment to *koinonia* has influenced the ecumenical gains made between Anglicans and Lutherans in the twentieth and twenty-first century. They set such gains in the wider context of other ecumenical success not only as a means to deeper mission but as a means to healing.

The mission of God from which the church springs and to which the church is called is, and always has been, witness amidst diversity and pluralism. In chapter eight, Clare Amos and Daniel Sperber explore interreligious dynamics particularly focused on the sacred space of Jerusalem. Reflection on Psalms 48 and 87, as well as a reading of Jewish understandings of sacred space or the holiness of place, raises powerful questions about understandings of God's revelation of God's self and the call of religious communities amidst competing claims to truth and land.

In chapter nine, Lucinda Mosher and Najah Nadi Ahmad provide an interreligious reading of chapters one through four, seven, and eight. They believe it is time and that it is possible to have a "candid interreligious conversation about witness and mission." Formation for witness, they suggest, is best done in "interreligious fellowship." From their experience with scriptural study between Christians and Muslims, and echoing earlier chapters in this volume, they see it as a path to deeper understanding and constructive disagreement.

Samy Fawzy Shehata (a Christian) and Nayla Tabbara (a Muslim) read and review chapters five through eight, picking up the themes of friendship, peace, and generosity as important not only for this volume but for their work and understanding of interreligious witness. They write chapter ten from the perspective of Egyptian Anglicanism and the interreligious work of the Lebanese-based Adyan foundation. From that experience, and the perspective of devotion to God, they give examples of principles and priorities that make a real difference on the ground and in people's lives.

The final chapter of this book ends where we would like our readers' thinking to begin. Think about your own context, think about the ministry you are involved in and the ministries around you. As believers continuing to discern the mission of God, take this book as an opportunity for deeper discernment as you "prepare your minds for action" and "set all your hope on the grace that Jesus Christ will bring you when he is revealed" (1 Pet. 1:13).

1

Discipleship in the Mission of God

Robert S. Heaney and John Kafwanka K

> *In him you . . . heard the word of truth, the gospel of your salvation . . .*
> (Eph. 1:13)

In this chapter, we will lay out an understanding of life-giving mission as a call to intentional lifelong formation. In hearing from scripture, this call for mission as discipleship begins in God's own proclamation of God's grace. In response to this divine grace, revealed in the person and work of Christ, humans discern the mission of God first through gratitude for God's work. Anglicanism's five marks of mission are one way to think about, frame, and resource discipleship in the mission of God. Lest we repeat the mistakes of the past, mission formation and discernment need to take place in the context of intercultural study and intercultural partnership. The four priorities of vision, accountability, solidarity, and collaboration are identified as ways in which best practice in such intercultural fellowship can be found.

Hearing Scripture

Reading Ephesians chapter one is like stepping into an overfull and overflowing praise service. Long, breathless sentences praise the work of God. Praise tumbles forth as God's love spills over into creation as blessing, adoption, salvation, and re-creation. Ephesians begins in beautifully poetic praise, a hymn to the grace of God. Here is the fountainhead. Here is where our story as God's Church for God's world begins. The Church is the fruit of God's mission.

The first human missional act, called forth and modeled by a text like Ephesians, is worship (Eph. 1:3). The Church begins in gratitude for what God has done in God's world through Christ. Children of God, through the indwelling of the Holy Spirit, become children of God's promise for the renewal of all creation. The Holy Spirit that dwells in our hearts and in Christ's Church is the divine gift that moves us toward God's promise and is itself a foretaste of God's promise (Eph. 1:14). In a sense, then, we can say that the Church's entrance into God's mission begins in liturgy. It begins in praise and worship. It begins in recognizing and discerning the work of the triune God. It is no surprise, therefore, that the first of Anglicanism's five marks of mission is *proclamation*.

Five Marks of Mission

1. To proclaim the Good News of the Kingdom
2. To teach, baptize, and nurture new believers
3. To respond to human need by loving service
4. To seek to transform unjust structures of society, to challenge violence of every kind and to pursue peace and reconciliation
5. To strive to safeguard the integrity of creation, and sustain and renew the life of the earth

---

First and foremost, this proclamation is God's own proclamation. Ephesians underlines this by telling us that God's choice to call a people to God's self predated the foundations of the earth (Eph. 1:4–6)! God proclaims God's grace before the world even exists. The first mark of mission is, indeed, proclamation. It is God's own proclamation of God's self, and this grace-filled proclamation that remains even in the face of human sin. If those first reading the letter to the Ephesians pictured the universe as a series of levels of reality or steps toward reality, then the message here is that God, in Christ, has lifted his people high into the place of heavenly blessing (Eph. 1:3). This blessing and this forgiveness of sin (Eph. 1:7–8) through the sacrificial death of Christ is achieved by God and is a divine gift. God proclaims God's love for humans "according to the riches of God's grace" (Eph. 1:7) and according to God's "good pleasure." In other words, God's love for God's people and God's mission of salvation comes from the very heart of God.

The genesis of God's mission begins in God's heart of eternal love. It is God that makes us a people. It is God that makes us God's possession or inheritance (Eph. 1:11). Because of the eternal love of God and God's work to form us as God's people, we are called to live for love (the third mark of mission). The highest calling of those who have received this eternal love of God is to strive for a life that is not centered on gain or preferment but is a life that is dedicated to "the praise of God's glory" (Eph. 1:12). This is both a challenge and an honor. Yet it is God's call upon God's church, "marked with the seal of the promised Holy Spirit," that is the "pledge" of what is yet to come (Eph. 1:13–14; see Acts 2:33). These images may point to baptism. Believers are "sealed" or "marked" in the Spirit as they are called into a life of formation and into a mission pilgrimage toward that day when what has been revealed in part will be more fully revealed in the presence of God (the second mark of mission).

The climax of Ephesians chapter one is found in verses 9 and 10. God has made known God's will ("the mystery") that, in Christ, God's intent is for the healing of creation (the fifth mark of mission). In his ministry, Jesus fulfills the will of God. Jesus is, therefore, the answer to his own prayer that God's will would be done "on earth as in heaven" (Matt. 6:10). In his own body and ministry, it is as if Christ brings heaven and earth together. No wonder, then, that Ephesians chapter one looks to the end of time and sees Christ "sum up" or "gather together" heaven and earth. What Christ began in his earthly ministry will be brought to fulfillment at the end times.

Despite this wonderful vision of God's proclamation to the world before the world's creation, in the creation of the world, and in its redemption through Christ, the church has often fallen short in its proclamation of such world-shaping grace. The church has been guilty of mission malpractice. Tragically, such malpractice has been enacted sometimes by those who have called themselves "missionaries." Those who claim to follow Jesus Christ have been guilty of sins that include cultural superiority, imperialism, greed, racism, sexism, and homophobia. There are many and complex reasons for such malpractice. It is our conviction, however, that a key reason for such malpractice lies in being formed within a faulty theology of mission. Given the expansive view of God's mission set before us in Ephesians, what does it mean to speak of discipleship in the mission of God?

The Anglican Communion's *Intentional Discipleship and Disciple-Making: An Anglican Guide for Christian Life and Formation* ties together the mission of God and intentional discipleship.[1] That document states clearly:

> [F]rom the study of Scriptures, the life of the early Church, and the witness of different Christian traditions over two thousand years . . . *intentional* discipleship and the regular practice of making disciples are central to our understanding of salvation, mission, and [church].[2]

Discipleship cannot be understood independent of Christ's mission to God's world.[3] The church is the community that has met the risen Christ (Eph. 1:20) and been converted to him as missionary disciples.[4] Called into God's grace, we are called into God's life-giving intent for humanity. Converted, and converting, we seek to center our lives on the crucified and risen Christ who was flung to the margins by the powerful. In centering on Christ, we

---

1. John Kafwanka and Mark Oxbrow, eds., *Intentional Discipleship and Disciple-Making: An Anglican Guide for Christian Life and Formation* (London: Anglican Consultative Council, 2016), 3.
2. Kafwanka and Oxbrow, *Intentional Discipleship*, 3.
3. Kafwanka and Oxbrow, *Intentional Discipleship*, 23.
4. Kafwanka and Oxbrow, *Intentional Discipleship*, 33; *Evangelii Gaudium*, 120, http://w2.vatican.va/content/francesco/en/apost_exhortations/documents/papa-francesco_esortazione-ap_20131124_evangelii-gaudium.html.

come to the source of grace and life who was marginalized by the empire. In coming to Christ, there is, then, also always a going because the Christ at the center of the church is simultaneously the Christ of the margins. In centering our lives on Christ, through scripture and sacrament, we are turned around to the world and to the world's margins (the fourth mark of mission). It is in being drawn to the risen Christ and being sent to the world that we are the church. The church catholic proclaims, at all times and in all places, its sustaining source as the grace of God found in Jesus Christ. This corporate proclamation should resource and sustain believers in their communities as people who can give expression and voice to this hope we have in our hearts (Eph. 1:18).

What would it mean, in your context, to consider the five marks of mission to be five marks of *formation*? Such formation or discipleship would focus on discerning God's call in preparing the baptized to (1) articulate the faith, (2) teach one another the faith, (3) respond faithfully to the needs in the community, (4) faithfully challenge all forms of injustice, and (5) faithfully protect the environment. Formation for mission begins with God's own proclamation of God's grace as we are drawn together in worship (the first and second marks of mission). In this proclamation, by the power of the Holy Spirit, we are changed and called into being the embodiment of God's hope (the Good News) in our communities. The baptized give voice to this hope as the community of Christ. The first chapter of Ephesians provides us with the key elements of what this hope is that might, in turn, further define the next four marks of mission. In testifying to the mission of God, we are called to tell the world:

- We know forgiveness because of the eternal love of God found in the person and cross of Jesus Christ (Eph. 1:7–8). This grace is God's invitation to discipleship and the source for Christian growth (the second mark of mission).
- We seek to live lives not determined by our own desires but by the love and grace of God (Eph. 1:12). This is made manifest in the world when we serve others (the third mark of mission).

- We are people of hope because the good news of Jesus means friendship with God (Eph. 1:13–14, 20–23). This hope in the Lord of lords has broken into human history and is the ground for unveiling, challenging, and working toward life-giving change in the face of injustice (the fourth mark of mission).
- We are children of the "God who created all things" (Eph. 3:9) and we seek to be people known by our love for one another (Eph. 1:15–16; 2:7–10). That love is practiced in communities that face the harsh realities of ecological degradation. Love and care for one another means love and care for all God's creation (the fifth mark of mission).

Questions for Reflection

Take a moment to reread Ephesians chapter one. Reflect on the following questions.

1. Gratitude is at the heart of the church's witness in and to the world. Write down, speak aloud, or sing out what you are thankful to God for today. Look carefully at verses 1–6. What does the author give thanks to God for? How does that compare to what you prioritize in your praise? How can verses 1–6 enrich your own gratitude to God?

2. In verses 7–14, there are powerful life-giving themes. Read these verses slowly and identify the gifts that God gives to God's people. How do you understand these gifts and how do you explain them in your setting?

3. What is your prayer for the church of Jesus Christ in your context and beyond? In Ephesians chapter one, the emphasis is given to the work of God in bringing salvation to the world (vv. 1–14). Praise begins with deep realization that mission is the work of God. God is the missionary God. In verses 15–19, attention turns to praise of God for the witness of the church in Ephesus. What ministry of the church do you give particular thanks for and why? How do verses 17–19 change your prayer for the church, and how would that prayer change the priorities for the church's ministry in your context?

4. The power of God that raised Christ from the dead (vv. 20–23) is the same power that brings renewed life (2:4–5). Where do you see signs of resurrection and renewal in your community? Where is resurrection needed? Spend time praying for new life in your community.

Hearing Each Other

God's Own Proclamation

A young man named Ben was born into a very religious family and was himself zealous in his religion. He took it upon himself to start converting his Christian schoolmates to his religion. His strategy was to study and master the Bible from the beginning to the end so that he could convince his Christian friends, most of whom had very scant knowledge of the Bible, to abandon Christianity and own his faith. The strategy worked. He managed to convince some of them with his prolific knowledge of the Bible. However, one day, as he read the Gospel of John, he found something unexpected in chapter 14:15–18, which reads:

> If you love me, you will keep my commandments. And I will ask the Father, and he will give you another Advocate, to be with you forever. This is the Spirit of truth, whom the world cannot receive, because it neither sees him nor knows him. You know him, because he abides with you, and he will be in you. I will not leave you orphaned; I am coming to you.

He was struck by this passage speaking about God sending the Holy Spirit and abiding among the disciples. The young man wanted to find out more, so he started attending a Christian fellowship. He was warmly received. More and more he was drawn to the fellowship. He was drawn to studying the Bible with an open, listening heart and not for purposes of proselytism.

Ben's father was the religious leader in the community. He grew suspicious of his son's Christian activity. On three occasions, during the holidays at home, his father asked his son if he had become a Christian. On three occasions the son denied it. His father asked him a fourth time. Ben confessed that he had become a Christian.

Counting the Cost

At that moment his father, visibly angry, told his son that he was no longer his child. For the next twenty years or so, the young man experienced all kinds of harassment. Under the direction of his own father, he endured severe beatings at the hands of his close family members and former coreligionists. On one occasion, he was stripped naked and so badly beaten and injured that he was left for dead. Through decades of degradation, suffering, and ostracization, he was supported by Christian fellowship and leaders in the Christian community.

Thirty years passed before Ben would see his father again. After all these years, he was to meet him on his deathbed. Visiting him in the hospital, it was Ben's hope that he would be reconciled with his father. It remains an unrealized hope. Speaking about this whole experience, Ben has this to say: "I bear no grudge whatsoever against any member of my family, not even my father—I only have love for them and they all know that. In fact, I am grateful for the experience I have gone through because it brought to life the love of Jesus Christ for me and the whole of humanity." The testimony here is love.

The Mission Is God's

Not every follower of Christ will be called to endure what Ben has endured. However, his testimony speaks to the emphasis found in Ephesians 1:4–6: the mission is God's. God is the agent of God's mission. In your context, are there stories or testimonies that tell of people coming to faith in Christ seemingly independent of human witness?

Miriam lives in a village with no Christians. By chance one day she heard a radio program about Jesus. Over the weeks she tuned into the show and learned that the story was from the Gospel of Mark. She learned of a village prophet who could drive out demons and forgive sin. She heard of a Jesus who cared for the poor and healed the sick and was opposed by religious leaders. In his stories and parables, she recognized a teacher with wisdom and compassion. Creatures and creation submitted to his healing command. His followers loved him, and many villagers eagerly sought him out. Yet, in the end, he would not compromise with the religious leaders and he was betrayed. She wept as she listened to the narrator read Mark chapter 15:

> Then the soldiers led [Jesus] into the courtyard of the palace. . . . And they clothed him in a purple cloak; and after twisting some thorns into a crown, they put it on him. And they began saluting him, "Hail, King of the Jews!" They struck his head with a reed, spat upon him, and knelt down in homage to him. After mocking him, they stripped him of the purple cloak and put his own clothes on him. Then they led him out to crucify him (vv. 16–20).

That evening Miriam had a dream. She dreamt that a stranger came to her village. He walked down the hill into her village in the cool of the evening. As he walked, he stopped to greet the elders and those who were enjoying evening conversation together. He continued to walk deeper into the village, passing home after home and greeting person after person. Eventually, this stranger came to Miriam's house. He knocked on the door. Miriam opened the door, and he greeted her by name. He said nothing more but turned around and started to walk back to the village entrance. She knew she should follow him, but she hesitated. What would others say? She was unmarried and this man was a stranger. But she had a sense that she knew who he was. He paused and looked back at her. Again, she hesitated. As he continued to walk away from her, she ran after him. She caught up with him at the entrance to the village. Again, she hesitated. He looked at her and held out his hand. As he did so, she saw the nail print and knew that it was Jesus who was calling her to follow him.

Miriam became a follower of Jesus. She wrote to the radio station that broadcast the stories from Mark's Gospel and eventually she received a smuggled Bible. Today, she leads a small Bible study group in her village.

Questions for Reflection

5. How do both of these stories, based on real life testimony, shape or change how you understand "mission"?
6. Read Ephesians 1 again.
7. After reading the testimonies of Ben and Miriam, how has your reading of the text changed? What do you notice that you did not notice the last time you read it?
8. How would you tell the story of your own faith journey in the light of Ben's and Miriam's stories?
9. How would you tell the story of your own faith journey in the light of Ephesians 1?
10. Is there someone in your family or community that you can share your story with?

The story of scripture and the story of believers testify to the same truth—the mission is God's. Therefore, we need each other to discern God's work and will. For no one culture, people, or language is sufficient to express the richness of God's grace. The mission of God is always intercultural and, thus, being a disciple of Jesus means learning across cultures and across differences. How are we to partner in such discipleship? How can we discern the mission of God and learn together even amidst difference? In the rest of this chapter, we provide some guidelines for discerning and practicing "partnership" as a means to intercultural discipleship.

The term "partnership" can evoke practices and patterns of unequal and unhealthy relationships that result in paternalism and dependence. However, if properly understood, it still communicates the essence of being and working together in mutual interdependent relationship.[5] By definition, partnership implies a relationship between or among individuals or groups of people or organizations who collaborate to achieve a common task or vision. In Christian terms, partnership is about being sisters and brothers in fellowship and love. That is to say, Christian partnerships are based on adequately

---

5. See chapter seven on communion.

conceived and healthy relationships. In the next section, we identify four characteristics of life-giving mission partnership.

Hearing the Spirit

[W]e are made to live in a delicate network of interdependence with one another, with God and with the rest of God's creation.

—Desmond Tutu[6]

Shared Vision: A Spiritual Exercise

Central to partnership in bearing witness to Christ is the importance of a shared common vision of God's holistic love (mission) for the world. Thus, holistic Christian witness—proclamation of the Good News in word and deed in every sphere of life—is what Christians are called to as followers of Jesus. This may require those in mission relationships to identify specific areas as opportunities to serve God together. In the early church, the support for a common goal was a practical way of establishing unity across local churches. Community support for common goals remains a means to partnership today.

Reflect on your own faith community. Who do you share common vision with? Are there already existing partnerships with outsiders? To what extent have you prayed with partners and built a common vision together? Sharing a vision for mission is not simply about practical priorities. It is a call to spiritual discernment. It is the call to listen to the Spirit. Invite members of the partnership and/or your local community into the following spiritual exercise.

- Read Ephesians 1:2–4 slowly together. Invite different voices to read the text and, if appropriate, invite members to read the text in different languages.
- Sit together in silence.

---

6. Desmond Tutu, *An African Prayer Book* (New York: Doubleday, 1995), xiv.

- Reread Ephesians 1:2–4 and, if possible, again invite different voices to read.
- Sit, again, in silence.
- Invite members of the group to speak aloud phrases or words that spoke to them.
- After more silence, invite members of the group to picture, in their minds, their home community. Ask them to walk around their community in their mind's eye. What do they see? What do they smell? Who do they meet? Finally, invite members to envisage themselves returning to their homes.
- Keep silence.
- Now invite members to imagine that Jesus knocks on their door. Jesus calls them to walk around the community with him. Where does Jesus go? What does Jesus show them? Who does Jesus meet? Who does Jesus talk to?
- Keep silence.

After this exercise, make sure you have enough time to gently debrief with the group. What was their experience of walking around the community? What was their experience of walking around the community with Jesus? As the group shares, what common themes emerge? Is there a common vision that Christ is calling the group to? It may be important to repeat this exercise several times so that group members feel more comfortable doing it and more open to the Spirit's leading. Important too is a commitment to testing any vision that emerges in relationships of mutuality and respect.

Mutual Accountability and Respect

In a relationship each part is accountable to the other. In Christian partnerships all the parties are first and foremost accountable to the triune God, whose mission it is that they seek to take heed of or participate in. For many, relationship accountability tends to be "one way," is often about money, and requires the "receivers" to be accountable to the "givers." This is the case because, in many relationships, money is regarded as the only resource that is given and/or received. This puts undue emphasis on money as the focal point in the partnership at the expense of other equally (if not more) important resources.

A spirit of mutuality means that all parties to a partnership must be accountable to one another. God calls us to a common communion and God may call us to a specific common witness and task. Because the mission is God's, the Spirit is calling all partners to a deeper sense of God's presence and grace (Eph. 1:2–3). Regardless of material possessions, no assumptions can be made about who in the partnership needs more of God's grace and God's word. All come before God as children of God. Equality is not diminished by the difference either in resources or personal disposition. As already observed, partners will bring different gifts to the task or relationship, but they are of equal importance. This is essential in understanding the meaning of Christian mission partnership as discipleship.[7]

Receiving and Giving in Solidarity

In the New Testament there is evidence of healthy models of mission partnership. Particularly instructive is Paul's relationship with the Philippian Church. That partnership was not restricted to money but rather included other aspects, such as emotional, moral, and prayer support. Thus, Paul would say, "It is right for me to think this way about all of you, because you hold me in your heart, for all of you share in God's grace with me, both in my imprisonment and in the defense and confirmation of the gospel" (Phil. 1:7–8). It is evident in Paul's letter that although money was important, it was not the only or primary resource for accomplishing the task at hand, namely proclaiming the good news of the kingdom.

In 2 Corinthians 8 and 9, Paul articulates the nature of Christian sharing that results in building one another up as an expression of human solidarity, especially among Christians as the body of Christ (1 Cor. 12). For Christians, partnership means that we do not only share in celebrating the "profits" but also the challenges and opportunities of our brothers and sisters, for it is a

---

7. 2 Corinthians 8:13–15.

question of "a fair balance. As it is written, 'The one who had much did not have too much, and the one who had little did not have too little'" (2 Cor. 8:14–15).

The partnership principles mentioned above are vital for mission relationships today. All are invited to embrace them as a means to deeper discernment of God's work in God's world. The call to collaboration and partnership as discipleship is not simply for the sake of unity, but also for the sake of the gospel.

Collaboration

We need each other to discern, enter into, and experience the richness of God's mission. This lesson lay at the heart of Paul's relationship with the Church of Philippi. No one has all that is needed to fulfill the missionary mandate of the church. All Christians are called to discern how they are to take heed of and participate in God's mission. The mission of God flows from the love of God into creation and re-creation. God creates communities and Communion to testify to this love across the world and across cultures. As Paul needed support to plant churches in Macedonia and Thessalonica, so today we need Communion partners in Buenos Aires and Busan, Cape Town and Chennai, Lagos and London, New Delhi and New York. In discerning God's mission across differences, we share resources and, by the mercy of God, grow deeper into God's grace and discipleship. Archbishop Rowan Williams is correct: "[T]here are things we shall never know about Jesus Christ and the written Word unless we hear from and see what they do in ever-new contexts."[8] As you and your community work with partners or work to establish partnerships, reflect together on these important questions:

- What words and priorities define "partnership" in my context?
- How do we understand the relationship between partnership and discipleship?

---

8. Foreword in Andrew Walls and Cathy Ross, eds., *Mission in the 21st Century: Exploring the Five Marks of Global Mission* (Maryknoll, NY: Orbis, 2008), xi.

- If God is the agent of God's mission, what priorities must be primary in a partnership?
- If we were writing a partnership agreement, how would answers to these questions and other questions in this chapter impact the language we would use?

Most of what passes for "partnership" in the church has thrived on and maintains "donor-recipient" models that embed paternalistic and colonial attitudes and practices.[9] This has meant that mission agencies have often seen themselves as donors or suppliers while regarding the so-called "partner" as the "implementer" of a program designed by the former alone. Although the achievements may be celebrated by both, that does not make such a relationship a partnership. Even with a shift in language around the Communion, paternalistic practices, attitudes, and behavior largely remain unchanged. We have a long way to go in a deeper conversion to the God of love that calls us to deeper relationship with the source of all blessings.

Companion link relationships in the Anglican Communion are not exempt from these failures, as many continue to operate in the manner that is sustained by paternalism on the one hand and dependence on the other. Those who "give" feel perfectly justified to see themselves as the "good Samaritans" of the poor, while those who "receive" also feel justified seeing themselves as the poor who deserve help, especially support that comes from outside. At times it is those on the "receiving" end who would use their "situation" to manipulate the "giving partner." Sometimes "receivers" can "act poor" or present a negative image of themselves and those they purport to support in order to appeal to the emotions of their "partner." In the end, this is false testimony. It misrepresents the humanity and wealth of the "receivers" and it misrepresents the humanity and wealth of the "donors." It reduces all sides in the partnership to economic function. In contrast, the gospel declares

9. See Jonathan Barnes, *Power and Partnership: A History of the Protestant Mission Movement* (Eugene, OR: Pickwick, 2013), and Michael Bamwesigye Badriaki, *When Helping Works: Alleviating Fear and Pain in Global Missions* (Eugene, OR: Wipf and Stock, 2017).

that all are made in the image of God. All are in need of the grace of God. A partnership based on mutual testimony and honest sharing of circumstances and call has the potential to build up the body of Christ in holistic and life-giving ways. Partnership is a call to deeper discipleship. It is a call to renewed experience of God's grace.

There are (and will always be) those many genuine cases of people who have to rely on the hospitality and generosity of others. There is continued need to look at better ways of providing support that empowers people rather than demeans and "condemns" them to be perpetual "recipients." Labeling or characterizing people, nations, or regions as "developed" and "undeveloped" or "rich" and "poor" oversimplifies the world and may lead people astray in their discipleship. There are historical and structural complexities in the creation of poverty. Centuries of power abuse through imperialist and ecological exploitation compounded by unjust trading arrangements and poor governance have made many in the world vulnerable to poverty and disease. In contrast, the same power abuses, exploitation, trading arrangements, and poor governance have unfairly rewarded others from one generation to the next. The wealthy often comfort themselves with myths of being "self-made" women and men. They remain blind to the structural and inherited benefits they have received through the exploitation of God's children and God's creation. Such myths lead to deep spiritual blindness, pride, and paternalism. It is only in ongoing repentance and conversion that the church and Communion can move beyond this sin to just repair. Substituting new words for old words is not enough. Discipleship and fellowship in God's mission, grounded in renewed and renewing partnership, is a vital means to spiritual growth.

A Lesson from Anglican History

The Toronto Congress of 1963 is famous for its propagation of "Mutual Responsibility and Interdependence" (MRI). Warning those attending the congress, Archbishop Michael Ramsey said, "The Church that lives to itself will die by itself." This slogan became central to the work of the congress, appearing in the opening words of the Congress Message/Communiqué. This gathering brought together large numbers of the laity, the priesthood, and the episcopate in prayer and reflection to discern what "God was saying to the Church and her role in the World," and to consider how churches of the Anglican Communion could work together in mission and in common discipleship as the body of Christ.[10]

The Toronto Congress took place at a time of immense change when countries that were under colonial regimes were working for emancipation and a number had already become independent from European rule and exploitation. Church leadership remained largely in the hands of white missionaries, but change was already in the air and everyone smelled it! Most importantly, there was a sense at the congress that the church's mission in the world was somehow central to her existence and nature and that it was closely associated with practices of collaboration within the body of Christ. The congress gathering was seen very much as a call to responsible Christian discipleship. It was this understanding that discipleship is at the heart of mission that led the congress to adopt the concept of MRI. For example, commenting on his experience of the congress, the primate of Canada, the Most Rev. Howard H. Clark, said:

> We tried together to listen, through the addresses and sermons and discussions, to what God is saying to the Church and to the world. I know that for me it means that no longer can I sing of "You in your small corner and I in mine." In all I do in the service of God my brother is with me, whether he is Asian, African, European or Australian. His needs and opportunities become one judgement upon my work. Whatever task God is calling us to, if it is yours it is mine, and if it is mine it is yours. We must do it together—or be cast aside together, as God in his absolute freedom goes on by other means to use his Church in hastening his Kingdom.[11]

---

10. Anglican Congress and Eugene Fairweather, *Anglican Congress 1963: Report of the Proceedings* (Toronto: Editorial Committee Anglican Congress, 1963), xiii.

11. Anglican Congress, *Report of the Proceedings*, xiii.

It is very important to understand here that the Church is all of us together. All are called to be light and salt—not just Episcopalians or Anglicans but all Christian peoples in their diversity of language and accent, ethnicity and tribe, region and nationality, denomination and doctrine, gender and sexuality, so that together we can discern the breadth and depth of the love and grace of God toward the world and in the world.[12] Although not dependent on it, the credibility, efficacy, and effectiveness of God's mission in the world is not disconnected from the nature and quality of mission relationships and discipleship in the church and Communion. After all, Jesus said the quality of the disciples' internal relationships would make people know that they were his disciples.[13]

Questions for Reflection

11. If mutual responsibility is a Christian priority, who is it we are called to be in relationship with?
12. Who, in your context, belongs to the margins?
13. How do you partner in discipleship with those on the margins?
14. If mission partnership is a call to deeper discipleship, what attitudes and mindsets do you need to change as you are involved in local, intercultural, and international mission?

We only live once. We can only ever be at one place at one time. Our perspective is always limited. Our experience of God is always limited. We need others so that we can have a more expansive experience of the love of God. We need other people's experiences and perspectives to appreciate the vision of God for the world revealed in Christ. Discipleship is never a solitary vocation. Unless we are ready and willing to listen and learn, even from the knowledge and experience of those we have always taught and given to, we risk missing the opportunity to experience the missionary God in others.

---

12. See chapter seven on the importance of common ecumenical vision, and chapters nine and ten on the potential of deeper interreligious vision and collaboration.
13. John 13:34–35.

Let us not cut ourselves off from the work of God's spirit in others. Let us open ourselves to the missionary God who can surprise us and overturn our assumptions and presuppositions. Cross-cultural encounter/experience helps us to see and understand ourselves anew, it helps us to understand the scriptures anew, and it helps us to experience God anew. Archbishop Desmond Tutu put it well when he said:

> A totally self–sufficient human being is ultimately a sub-human. We are made for complementarity. I have gifts that you do not; and you have gifts that I do not. So we need each other to become fully human . . . and to realise the fullness of our potential. God is smart, making us different so that we will get to know our need for each other.[14]

The legacy of the Toronto Congress is unclear. Despite the rhetoric, the reality is that the Church continues to misunderstand the mission of God. The Church continues to emphasize its own agency and not the free sovereign work of God in God's world (Eph. 1). The past need not be the future. God calls us to be a people of hope. God calls us into relationship with God's self and God's world. Let us pray that a renewed understanding of discipleship in the mission of God can once more inspire better leadership and relationships to the glory of God.

Take a moment of silence and reflect on this chapter and what God has been revealing to you. After that silence, pray aloud the following prayer:

> God of grace and peace,
> visit your children with every spiritual blessing
> that we might know your love in our hearts,
> and your healing will for your Church and world,
> through the power of the Spirit gifted to your people by the risen
>   Christ.
> Amen.

---

14. Tutu, *African Prayer Book*, xiv.

2

Communion as the Discipline of Listening and Talking

Alan Yarborough and Marie Carmel Chery

As part of God's creation, each one of us is called to make the kingdom of God better known on earth. According to what gifts we received, we must work for the well-being of all. We do this through mission, and frequently in that mission we are called to leave our familiar comforts behind and go out into the world, so we can share in others' journeys. Because we cannot be everywhere at all times, nor can we be certain of the experiences of others, it is very important for us to allocate time to extend invitations and listen to people describe their situations from their own context. By listening carefully, we can better discern how we might become better equipped to serve God together.

God has asked us to love one another, not just in speech, but in truth and action (1 John 3:18). In this chapter we will explore the discipline of listening as we walk in the way of Christ toward the realization of God's vision for the world. We often mistakenly look at listening as the absence of action, but listening is indeed an activity requiring astute participation, particularly across differences between cultures, languages, experiences, identities, and opinions. Yet to persevere in the discipline of listening, especially as we seek to understand those who are different from us, we first listen to scripture. Throughout the biblical narrative we are reminded that we are a common people. We are all children of God. This God-given oneness is the basis for building healthier relationships and addressing the needs of the world we share together. As our chapter is titled "Communion as the Discipline of Listening and Talking," we seek to demonstrate how listening to scripture, to each other, and to the Spirit can help in working more efficiently for the common good of the whole body.

Hearing Scripture

> *But you are a chosen race, a royal priesthood, a holy nation, God's own people, in order that you may proclaim the mighty acts of him who called you out of darkness into his marvelous light. Once you were not a people, but now you are God's people; once you had not received mercy, but now you have received mercy.*
>
> (1 Pet. 2:9–10)

When we listen to scripture, the Spirit reveals to us something more about ourselves and about God. The best place for us to learn from and about God is in God's word. By hearing the scripture, we become better listeners. By becoming better listeners, we become better witnesses. For the people of God, scripture provides direction for life, inspiration for moving forward, and context for our faith. Indeed, if we can become a people that listens deeply, we will be a people that proclaims the savior who listened. We listen to scripture as inspiration and guidance for living out our call as followers of Jesus and people commissioned to build the kingdom.

First Peter 2:9–10 shows us that this call to witness begins in God's call on our lives. We are chosen by God to be God's witnesses:

> Who we are is integral to how we witness the good news. God invites us—as God's people have been invited in every generation—to be transformed into a sign, foretaste and instrument of the kingdom (or reign) of God. As sign, the church points to the creating, loving, healing, just and forgiving God of the scriptures, most clearly doing so in worship which marks it as a holy community of thanksgiving and praise. As foretaste, the church embodies in its life the value

of the reign of God, most clearly doing so in mutual love which marks it as a catholic (universal, all-inclusive) community service. As instrument, the church shares in God's mission in the world, most clearly doing so in deeds and words which mark it as an apostolic community of witness.[1]

First Peter 2:9–10 exhorts the people of God to proclaim the work of God's redemption. Witnesses, however, do not simply talk. They also listen deeply. The Church is called to listen deeply as a chosen people and to listen deeply to her Lord, who in his life and work made her a people ready to proclaim God's mighty acts. These mighty acts are seen clearest in the witness of Jesus.

As followers of Jesus, we are taken up into God's mission. This mission is shaped by the person and example of Jesus. God made an appeal to us to carry forth God's mission on earth, which scripture sums up as the work of "reconciliation." In this work of reconciliation, we are to "regard no one from a human point of view; even though we once knew Christ from a human point of view, we know him no longer in that way. So if anyone is in Christ, there is a new creation: everything old has passed away; see, everything has become new!" (2 Cor. 5:16–17). First Peter reiterates this message of oneness and newness in God. The old has been shaken off and a new reality emerges. The darkness has given way to light.

In Jesus, God showed us the way to love our neighbor (the Great Commandment, Mark 12:30–31), grant mercy (Luke 10:37), and be peacemakers (Matt. 5:9). First Peter reminds us that this mercy, this holiness, this light originates in God, and shines forth in us, as we are God's people. As 1 Peter calls us to proclaim God's goodness, we are reminded that witness is not just faithful speaking, but also faithful listening.

As people who are part of God's chosen race, shaped by what we have heard in scripture, we must listen to one another. We are one as God's creation

---

1. The Standing Commission for Mission of the Anglican Communion, "Establishment of MISSIO," 22, accessed August 12, 2019, https://www.anglican communion.org/media/108016/MISSIO-The-Standing-Commission-for-Mission -of-the-Anglican-Communion.pdf.

and we are one as God's new creation. God has achieved, in Christ, a new community and calls us to listen for deeper signs of that community. Thus, we are called to seek out opportunities to be in deeper reconciling community. In listening to one another, this God-given community deepens our spiritual awareness and brings the healing of the body closer. We are called to be with one another and we are called to heal one another. Adequately addressing the needs and hurts in the world requires working together—after all, Jesus commissioned disciples multiple times in the Bible (Luke 10; Matt. 28:16–20). Working together requires both listening and participating in communication, as Jesus and his disciples embodied when sharing and hearing parables throughout his ministry.

When it is time to speak out, everybody wants to be heard. Listening to others is one of God's qualities, as we learn from the Gospel of John when Jesus raises Lazarus to life (John 11:41–42), and as we see in Jesus when he responds to his followers' questions. We need to listen to each other so that we can know where our help can be most effective, and so that we can better know what actions to take to build community with one another. As Christians, we are chosen not because we are better than anyone else, but because God is sovereign and wants us to show who God really is to others by commissioning us to share God's love, God's mercy, and God's grace everywhere.

First Peter helps us approach the discipline of listening by pointing to the oneness we share in God. Christians are now spread around the world. We speak a vast array of languages and incorporate a wide range of cultural norms into the ways we practice the faith. The exercise of Christian worship, the organization of church community, and the ministries carried out by the church take different forms in contexts from South Bend to Rome, from Haiti to South Sudan, from Ecuador to India. Yet 1 Peter tells us that while cultural and geographical boundaries persist, we should not allow these demarcations to separate us from God and from each other. Rather, God reconciles people to God's self and in doing so makes divided peoples a united people ("a chosen race"). First Peter is saying there is something that binds us together, and that something is the work of God, in Christ.

The emphasis on oneness calls us to pay attention to what we have in common in our relationships with others, no matter the differences that exist between us. As we will explore in the next section, we must seek and learn from those differences, but if we are to really connect with "the other" in our ministry, we must anchor ourselves in this idea of oneness with each other and oneness with God. Our shared faith and shared scriptures provide all of us with a common experience through which we can feel drawn to one another and far less distant than our nationality, culture, language, or identity may initially imply.

This means that as we each reflect on this passage, we know that others are reflecting on the same passage. These verses are a call to each one of us in whatever context we live. No matter who we are or where we are, we are called by this scripture to listen to God's mercy, to proclaim God's mercy, and to be reassured by God's mercy. Of course, carrying out the practice of listening in daily life is more difficult than when reflecting about it on our own. Whether our own desire to be heard before understanding others gets in the way of truly listening, or the differences between us appear so great as to distract us or tire us along the way, putting listening into practice may well be one of the most challenging actions we must take in order to fulfill Christ's commandment to love one another (John 15:12–17).

It is true that though we all have access to the same scripture, our experiences may guide what we are hearing in that scripture and alter how we apply the lesson in our own lives. Likewise, what we hear in scripture may change as we grow older and gain new experiences. The same passages from the Bible can teach us different truths that are not mutually exclusive. However, it still holds true that the scripture serves as a common bond between us, and we may use this scripture and our diverse understandings of it to identify and uphold our common foundation on which we can build communion.

Even if we struggle through our practice of listening to others, we should remember the mercy God grants us when we do not listen. Moreover, we are not the only ones to doubt, to be hard of hearing, or to fall short of understanding God's call. Hence, the stories where Jesus exhibits patience with his disciples—repeating if necessary the message (John 21:15–17)—are signs to remember that we do not know everything and that we must take great care to listen. As we are called by God, so we are supported by God. God gifts us with patience and reassurance amidst our frustrations, misunderstandings, and errors. We know the mercy of God even when we do not listen attentively.

Questions for Reflection

1. First Peter 2:1–3 tells us that if we have "tasted" God's mercy, then this should change our attitudes with each other. How has your experience of the mercy of God made you listen better to others?
2. Many did not listen to the message Jesus brought (1 Pet. 2:4–8). Why was Jesus rejected? In what ways do you feel his message is rejected today?
3. God, in Christ, brings people together (1 Pet. 2:10). In your context, how does the Church bring people together from different backgrounds? What are the challenges of deeper unity in your context?
4. What is it like for you to hear that you are chosen by God (1 Pet. 2:9)? When thinking about the people you are in relationship with, both those you get along with and those you do not, what is it like to hear that they are chosen by God?
5. We are not the only ones God has called to ministry. How is listening a critical part of our role in understanding God's call to the whole church?

Hearing Each Other

The priority of missionaries is to listen to God and to those they are called to serve. It is not to impose their own ideas. It is to help a community already in progress build itself up. It is important for both the visitor and the host to sit down and openly discuss the desired direction for the community. By sitting with the leaders of the communities, missionaries can better understand what the needs are so they can then define how to approach one another in partnership. Such a principle will include the additional responsibility of communicating to all parties—near and far. By hearing each other, people become more connected, which tends to dissuade deceit and manipulation. Thus, little by little, one relationship at a time, the world becomes more compassionate.

Marie Carmel Chery has a good friend who was sent to minister in a place with no formal buildings—neither church nor school. It was a young community. This friend, who we will refer to as Richard, already had some partners who were ready to support him in building a school. However, Richard wished they would help him build the church first, since he had been ordained as a minister in the church. The partners struggled to understand his desire. After a long period of listening and discussion, they decided to help him build the church, then the school. Today, it is one of the most beautiful communities of the diocese, and many lives have been changed through it. The partners, in turn, are proud of their work.

Questions for Reflection

6. How can ministers and missionaries know what is most useful to a community?

7. How does a church best learn and discern the needs of a local community?

8. In your context, are there ever tensions or disagreements between the church's vision for a community and other people's vision for the community? How are such problems resolved?

9. What do you think is a priority for seeking to discern God's mission in your context?

Richard's story demonstrates the need to listen to others in ministry and in partnership. We are called to listen to those we are called to serve. We may think that we understand the impact of our actions, but without listening deeply to the community, many unintended consequences emerge. Mission means following the Christ who listens. Mission means the sharing of grace that listens, a commitment always to learn from each other. As the saying goes, whoever gives, receives back. If you are blessed with money and you want to share some with the ones who don't have enough, it does not mean they have nothing to give back. You can receive from them things that are priceless. We have met people who have been completely transformed after being in touch with people living in different contexts. Even in the midst of suffering, our sisters and brothers have much to share in their resilience. Some may find their faith increases after visiting different places, some become stronger than before, some find their call to ordained ministry after sharing an ordained minister's journey. Openness of mind and humility are important in mission. When we keep in mind the one we are called to witness to, we can sit with others patiently and learn from their own reality. When love is above all, we are patient, open, humble. We can touch one another's lives and grow in confidence and mutual respect.

After the jostling ride from the airport, Ryan welcomed the calm of the open road outside of Port-au-Prince. This was his first time in Haiti. The arrival to the airport seemed familiar enough. But once his car hit the streets, the heated flash of *motos*, *tap taps*, *Madam Saras*, and trucks full of white sand transported him into what felt like a different world. This unfamiliarity he felt between himself and the world around him remained even as the environment became more rural on the way up Mon Kabrit, heading into the Central Plateau. He was traveling to a small community in one of the poorest regions of the country. At dusk, he arrived in the gated complex that would be his home for the week. In a town of 3,400 people, he was welcomed by a handful of greeters. Ryan quickly made friends with a young man, Ti Wil, who didn't waste time on pleasantries before making deals to produce custom bracelets for all of Ryan's family back home. After an evening group reflection, Ryan and some fellow travelers, along with Ti Wil and a few other local guys who could not speak English, enjoyed Prestige—the award-winning Haitian beer. Ryan had never heard of the beer before, yet it was something familiar.

When the sun rose early, the rapid heat and unfamiliar sounds of chickens and a woman's hands washing laundry got Ryan out of bed quickly. The landscape he could not see well the night before was suddenly in full display.

It was dry with few trees and wafts of smoke rising from a seemingly abandoned landscape. He was offered black grits for breakfast. Someone in the breakfast line ahead of him said it was their favorite dish in Haiti, but, nervously, he only took a partial scoop. But it really was delicious. For round two, he filled his plate and topped it off with fresh avocado. The women serving the food smiled and clapped at him. Ryan smiled. Had they eaten today? He turned away quickly. Poverty.

The morning activity was canceled, so Ryan stepped outside, finding Ti Wil waiting on the front steps. "Let me show you my house," he said. Could he go outside the complex? Was it safe? What would he see and how would he act? How much English did Ti Wil actually know? Ryan went anyway.

He saw houses made of concrete, and others built like flimsy lean-tos. Kids were everywhere. People kept yelling something at him. They smiled when he made eye contact, so he waved back. The walk was hot and long, up and down rocky ruts with few trees around. They reached Ti Wil's house, built like a lean-to. Over ten people were sitting around outside in the shade of a tall tree filled with fruits. Ryan saw the dirt, the leaves of the roof, the children sitting around and the old people too, all together, in the heat. He smelled something burning behind the structure. He felt the harsh rocks under the soles of his new tennis shoes and thought about the mosquitoes his hi-tech shirt was blocking, and the sunscreen on his face making him whiter than he already was. Then, he heard the cry of the youngest child there—just a few years old. He was sitting in his mother's lap, touching his mouth. Hunger. Despair. Poverty.

Ryan held back tears. "This is my family," Ti Wil said with a smile. Mom, cousins, brother and sister, grandfather. They all waved and smiled, except for the youngest child. Ryan stared at them and said, "What's wrong with him?" Ti Wil spoke in Creole, and Ryan did not understand. Should I give them something, he thought? Perplexed, he wondered what was wrong with the child. Ti Wil kept speaking in Creole and laughed. Ryan asked again, "What's wrong with him . . . is he okay?" Ti Wil, still smiling, looked back at Ryan. Jean Marie, the little crying boy, had just lost his first baby tooth.

Questions for Reflection

10. What resonated with you about Ryan's mood throughout this story? What experiences have you had that impact your mood and your sense of place?
11. What was Ryan listening to during moments of silence or when he was with people speaking a language he could not understand?
12. What would you say is the most significant moment in this relatively simple story and why? What did Ryan overlook during this experience?
13. What were Ryan's impressions of the space that he entered? Do you believe that his thoughts were different from those living in the local region? Why? How do you think his perspective might have changed?

When Alan Yarborough first went to Haiti, he traveled to relocate there, not just to visit. He believed his listening began well before he arrived at the airport. In the three months between graduation from his undergraduate college and when he moved to Cange, he took on the responsibility of reading as much as he could about Haiti—history, politics, culture. He read different accounts of humanitarian aid, and the writings of different Haitian political leaders. He tried to prime himself for the move, and yet still felt very much like Ryan when he arrived.

As we have observed, Ryan, and others like him, have clear preconceptions about Haiti and poverty. Listening across difference is difficult, and people are correct to focus on those differences to better understand how someone with a radically different experience from our own sees and comprehends the world, sees and comprehends justice, sees and comprehends God. But looking back, Alan believes he ended up feeling similar to Ryan when he arrived because he approached listening to and interacting with Haiti based on difference. Everything he read about Haiti he read with the narrow mindset that he was entering a place "over there" distant from anything he knew or was implicated in. Over time, Alan began to see that focusing exclusively on differences when listening and learning is akin to a ship coming into harbor without an anchor. He interpreted everything as a difference, which made him deaf at first to anything that he had in common with his hosts. Only once he recognized similarities between himself and those around him could he more deeply connect with others. Only by listening to and understanding these similarities with the people in Haiti could he better define and understand the differences. By engaging the similarities, like babies losing baby teeth, he drew closer to people, finding common ground on which to base conversations and help illuminate his own experience for them just as he was learning about theirs.

Hearing the Spirit

Once you were not a people, but now you are God's people; once you had not received mercy, but now you have received mercy.

(1 Pet. 2:10)

First Peter 2:10 declares that God has done a new thing. God has renewed his people that they might declare God's praise and receive God's mercy. Like a cool drink of water before singing, discerning the Spirit in the lives and words of others nourishes the witness of God's church. Both the biblical text and ministry experience prove that no one can have a blessed ministry by acting on his or her own. It is imperative to rely on the Spirit to bear good fruits. According to the Bible, the Spirit searches everything, even the depths of God (1 Cor. 2:10). It is our duty to listen to the Spirit before making any decision, for there is no better counselor. If we are aware of challenges that people in mission face, then, with the Spirit guiding us, our actions can better reflect the healing will of God.

How might listening to the Spirit serve as a support for ourselves as we engage the difficult work of listening? To help identify where and how the Spirit may be at work, we will share one spiritual exercise that you can take part in as a reflection on the primary selection of scripture explored in this chapter, 1 Peter 2:9–10. We will base this exercise on the Benedictine practice of *Lectio Divina*. This practice emphasizes the living qualities of scripture and the ability of scripture to provide different teachings for us depending on how and when we are listening to it.

Let us meditate on the presence of the Spirit. Isaiah 11:2 says: "The spirit of the LORD shall rest on him, the spirit of wisdom and understanding, the spirit of counsel and might, the spirit of knowledge and the fear of the LORD." This describes the nature of the Spirit that rests on the new shoot and branch growing from the old stump, emphasizing the qualities of God's new creation. Remember that you have the same Spirit sent to you as the counselor whose mission is to guide you.

The Spirit of the Lord. When resting upon us, the Spirit allows us to transcend the impossible. Envisage going somewhere and transforming a hopeless place into a wonderful one. Remember that the Spirit is there before you arrive and will remain after you are there. How happy and reassured can we be if we only keep this in mind!

The Spirit of wisdom and understanding. Wisdom is the capacity to make decisions according to God's will. Mission is not, then, just about tangible outcomes but about how well we are realizing a deeper connection and oneness with God, each other, and with all of creation. Wisdom tells us what to do and understanding allows us to know why we need to do it. If we want to be wise, we have to wake early and hear the word of God (Isa. 50:4–5).

The Spirit of counsel and might. Throughout the Old Testament, whenever a person of God had to do something, they went to inquire of God before making any decision. There were at least three ways God answered—by dreams (Gen. 31:10–13), by the *Urim* and *Thummim* (Exod. 28:29–30), or by the prophets (1 Sam. 9:9). The fullest manifestation of God's presence and will has come to us in Christ (Heb. 1:1–2), and the church has been gifted with Christ's Spirit (Rom. 8:9). We have treasure in jars of clay, to show that the surpassing power belongs to God and not to us (2 Cor. 4:7). We can do mighty things in mission if we seek the will of the Lord through the Spirit who is already in us. We have to be wise enough to begin by the Spirit, and not be hindered by the flesh (Gal. 3:3). May we acknowledge how blessed we are to be witnesses of the Almighty God!

The Spirit of knowledge and the fear of the Lord. Knowing the Lord means we are obedient to God's will. Such obedience will bring such fear of the Lord, and it is said, the "fear of the LORD is the beginning of knowledge—fools despise wisdom and instruction" (Prov. 1:7). When we remember that we are called to witness for the Lord, we will do our best to let such Spirit work in us. We need to express such profound gratitude through obedience while staying in communion with God. Hearing the Spirit will bring us to do mighty things for the glory of the Lord. Build moments of thanksgiving into your relationships as well, allowing yourself to share what you are grateful for, and take time to listen to what others are thankful for as well. After becoming aware of why the Spirit is there, we hope you will hunger for hearing the spirit. This will make a huge difference in your ability to engage in relationships.

We will now begin the *Lectio Divina* exercise, which will require you to slowly read the same passage four times with the goal of listening to the scripture and the Spirit. Each reading of the passage will take a particular framing. Normally *Lectio Divina* follows the process of reading, meditating, praying, and contemplating on a single piece of scripture. For our exercise, we will follow four not so dissimilar steps: *identifying, reflecting, praying,* and *contextualizing.* As you work through this, know that others from different backgrounds, cultures, and contexts than you are working with this same passage.

> But you are a chosen race, a royal priesthood, a holy nation, God's own people, in order that you may proclaim the mighty acts of him who called you out of darkness into his marvelous light. Once you were not a people, but now you are God's people; once you had not received mercy, but now you have received mercy. (1 Pet. 2:9–10)

Identify. The goal of this first reading is simply to identify different elements in the text. Which parts of the text are you being called to give more attention? Do not analyze why these are standing out, just listen for them. Read slowly and aloud 1 Peter 2:9–10. Make a note of which words or phrases comfort you, which words startle or surprise you, and which words motivate you. Note parts of the text, if any, that make you uncomfortable or intimidated. Note any parts of the text that are unclear. You may repeat out loud any of these phrases or words from the text that particularly struck you.

Reflect. The goal of this second reading is to reflect more on why you are reacting to the text the way that you are. For the parts that startle, intimidate, or make you uncomfortable, say out loud why each part makes you feel this way. For the parts that comfort or motivate you, say out loud why you feel comforted or motivated, and what you feel motivated to do. If there are any parts that are unclear, read the passage again once or twice out loud, alternating your speed each time and reflecting on which words you place emphasis. Now read the text again (silently if you wish). Take your time with this reading, savoring each point in the text where you sense a reaction, and allow space in the exercise for the text to speak to you in deeper and less apparent ways. It is okay if parts of the passage remain unclear.

Pray. The goal of this third reading is to imagine your life and this world as if this passage were truly realized. Read the passage aloud again, but imagine the passage as if the things that are mentioned in the text—being a part of a royal and holy nation, proclaiming God's goodness, light overtaking darkness, people united as God's people, receiving mercy—are things that you are praying for in your own life and in the lives of others. Pause after this reading and sit in silent reflection for five minutes. Try to calm your mind and limit your own thinking. Allow the space around you and the text in front of you to continue speaking.

Contextualize. The goal of the fourth and final reading of the passage is to focus on the word "you." When you read through the passage again, consider to what extent you feel included in the intended audience of the passage. In other words, to what extent do you feel like the "you" in the passage includes yourself, or do you feel that the text is speaking to another group of people?

Once you finish this reading, think about others who are reading it but in different contexts than yours—these others may have a different socioeconomic status, may speak a different language, or may live in a different culture. How does this knowledge change how you read the text and draw comfort from the passage?

As you conclude your reading of this chapter and the reading of scripture, we offer you this closing prayer:

> Almighty and everlasting God,
> we thank you for your mercy and the gift of service you grant us.
> We thank you for your Spirit sent to guide us. We pray that we might see your image in all those we minister to and all those we meet in this life.
> May we be able to hear when you speak so we can be your witnesses among all your sons and daughters.
> In the midst of misunderstanding, may your unconditional love help us move forward. May your will be done in our lives and in the lives of all your children.
> In Jesus's name we pray. Amen.

3

Communion as Disagreeing Well

Sarah Hills and Deon Snyman

Hearing Scripture

The Emmaus Road (Luke 24:13-43)

Reconciliation is at the core of our gospel life (2 Cor. 5:14–20). Reconciliation is about renewing relationships in order to live better together—with God, self, others, and the earth. Reconciliation is not about agreement. It is about "loving our enemies" (Matt. 5:44). "Disagreeing well," therefore, becomes a key step in any journey of reconciliation. To walk alongside others, even in disagreement, begins with the first step of understanding ourselves and our stories. It is in such walking together, listening together, and understanding together that relationships, once broken, can start to heal.

In this chapter, we will explore "disagreeing well"—what it means, how to attempt it, and where it takes us. It is important at the outset to discuss disagreeing well in the overall context in which it has to take its place. That is to say, it is but one step in a journey toward that seemingly elusive goal of reconciliation. Reconciliation is a complex, messy, but always hopeful goal that involves:

- Learning how to disagree well
- Radical relating, which is vulnerable and trusting
- Authentic being with self and others

- Being open to God's grace
- Searching together for justice, truth, forgiveness, peace, and restitution
- Restoring wholeness and healing
- Transformation

This list is not exhaustive but grew out of our reconciliation experience in South Africa and other places of conflict and postconflict. It is based therefore on praxis, following John de Gruchy's thinking:

> Reconciliation is, indeed, an action, praxis and movement before it becomes a theory or dogma, something celebrated before it is explained. . . . [R]econciliation is properly understood as a process in which we become engaged at the heart of the struggle for justice and peace in the world. That is why any discussion of reconciliation must be historically and contextually centered, a reflection on what is happening on the ground by those engaged in the process. Only then can we critically engage the rhetoric and practice of reconciliation.[1]

This chapter began in conversations overlooking False Bay, one of the most glorious views in South Africa. The grandeur of the Overberg Mountains and the sound of the waves became the backdrop to our attempts at disagreeing well as we discerned how and what to write together. Such a backdrop stands in stark contrast to the historical backdrop of our country's journey toward reconciliation through the turbulence of the apartheid era. In protest marches, in prophetic voices, and in outright resistance, Christians sought to make sense of their identities amidst the struggle for transformation. This journey toward transformation invoked and involved confusion, lament, and anger. The passage of Luke 24:13–43 suggested itself to us. On this journey from Jerusalem to Emmaus there is disagreement, confusion, disappointment, lament, honesty, anger, and, in the end, transformation. It is a journey starting

---

1. John W. de Gruchy, *Reconciliation: Restoring Justice* (London: SCM Press, 2002), 22.

from a place of pain and suffering, where the two travelers had witnessed or heard about a terrible event, the crucifixion and death of Jesus of Nazareth, the one whom they had "hoped . . . was the one to redeem Israel" (Luke 24:21).

We join them as the two are walking and talking. We are told they were "looking sad" (Luke 24:17). Jesus joins them and is not recognized. They are astonished to learn he does not seem to know what has been happening in Jerusalem. Sadness overtakes them and confusion begins. Cleopas reacts sarcastically to Jesus's question, replying, "Are you the *only* stranger in Jerusalem who does not know?" (Luke 24:18, emphasis added). They outline their loss, their tragedy, their confusion, and perhaps disbelief at what the women have told them. "They did not see him" at the tomb (Luke 24:23). In response, Jesus calls them "foolish" and "slow of heart" (Luke 24:25). These seemingly harsh words suggest Jesus is not "disagreeing well"! As readers of the story, we might have expected kinder words. "I'm sorry for your loss" or "May he rest in peace" would surely be more pastoral and appropriate. This, of course, is not the only time we find Jesus being blunt. Think of the cleansing of the temple and his furious response to the traders (John 2:13–16). We have here, in Luke 24, a first clue about what disagreeing well might mean. Disagreeing well begins with honest emotion. In this text Jesus enters robustly into disagreement with these pilgrims. Both sides accuse the other of being stupid. Here is an honest and frank exchange, not a mild papering over of real feelings. Disagreeing well is not about being polite or nice to each other. We see from this passage that there needs to be space for real emotion to be expressed, and some plain talking.

Jesus, all the way through this passage, models how to disagree well. He listens to their story but reminds them that there is another narrative, a different way of seeing things. He puts it in context for them and takes them back through the whole of God's story, "beginning with Moses and the prophets." He reinterprets his own story for them and helps them to remember it (Luke 24:27). Their response to this truth-telling and honest emotion is to invite Jesus to stay with them. It is significant that Jesus made initially as if to go on walking alone (Luke 24:28). People in a disagreement often need space to process what they have heard "the other" say. Jesus accepts, however, their urging to not only walk together but also to eat together. In the act of sitting at table and watching Jesus breaking and blessing the bread, "their eyes are opened, and they recognized him" (Luke 24:31). Jesus turns things upside down. He is the stranger, we are told earlier (24:18), and yet, here he is, playing host. They have known him previously as host, and now that he acts as host again, they see what they could not see on the road. Jesus does the unexpected, the counterintuitive, the surprising thing. The stranger becomes the guest and the guest becomes the host. Jesus shifts their perspective. He enables a new way of seeing and that is transformative for them. Immediately, the two get up and go straight back to Jerusalem to tell the disciples what had happened, that "the Lord is risen!" (24:33–34). As we read on, we find, however, that the transformation they experienced had not entered deeply into their hearts. Jesus needs to give them even more time and even more evidence.

> While they were talking . . . Jesus himself stood among them and said to them, "Peace be with you." They were startled and terrified and thought they were seeing a ghost. He said to them, "Why are you frightened, and why do doubts arise in your hearts? Look at my hands and my feet; see that it is I myself. Touch me and see." (Luke 24:36–39)

Learning how to disagree well does not happen quickly. The journey is long, and often fraught. Anger, sadness, lament, and frustration all play their part. It is only when these difficult but necessary emotions have been felt and expressed to "the other" that progress can be made. "Being human" together—feeling angry with each other, sharing the same physical space, walking, eating, and remembering together—are all part of what it means to disagree well. Being vulnerable, honest, and spending time in shared space are steps toward disagreeing well and steps toward reconciliation.

Questions for Reflection

1. What were the emotions being played out on this journey? To what extent were these emotions helpful?

2. What might have happened in this passage if Jesus had not reacted with honest anger? Are there times when we hide our true feelings? Why do we do that?

3. Why was the breaking of bread in this story important? What were the steps that led to this moment?

4. What did Jesus do to create a "safe enough space" for this difficult conversation to happen well? How can we create such spaces?

Hearing Each Other

Different Disagreement Responses

There are many different responses to disagreement. It is possible to respond with animosity, hostility, aversion, hate, or bitterness. The relationship between the United States of America and the Islamic Republic of Iran comes to mind as an example. Such a response to disagreement is not helpful and does not allow for relationship, fellowship, or living in peace together. Despite their initial disagreement, the walkers had a meal together after they reached Emmaus.

Some people decide to avoid expressing disagreement and pretend there is no conflict. This response is also not helpful, as the root causes of the disagreement are not addressed. The renowned peace researcher Johan Galtung reminds us that it is only possible for people to live in real peace with each other when the root causes of the disagreement are sufficiently resolved. The Emmaus walkers resolved their disagreement through talking about it.

Some people use quiet diplomacy as a response to disagreement. They agree not to criticize each other in public but engage with each other in private to resolve the disagreement. At the turn of the twentieth century, it became clear that the Zimbabwean state was committing gross human rights violations against its citizens. Despite Western condemnation, the South African and other African governments decided to follow a quiet diplomacy approach. They agreed not to publicly criticize the Zimbabwean government but rather raise their concerns in private meetings with Zimbabwean leaders.

The Zimbabwean government exploited this approach by labeling Western criticism as imperialist and ignoring privately made promises to African governments. The quiet diplomacy approach failed. It forestalled the desired change and contributed to the economic collapse of the state.[2] The disagreement in Luke 24:13–43 became public when it was included in Luke's Gospel and thereby assisted readers in better understanding Jesus's message.

Questions for Reflection

5. In your context, to what extent is "quiet diplomacy" helpful? What makes it helpful and what makes it unhelpful?
6. Can you think of examples from scripture of good diplomacy? Why were they effective and how did they bring about transformation?

Managing Disagreement Well

The Zimbabwean situation was not facilitated well and it had serious consequences. Regardless of the context, if life-giving community is to be nourished, disagreement must be managed well. We suggest at least four key steps to good disagreement.

First, it is necessary for the disagreeing parties to acknowledge to each other that they disagree. This acknowledgment will bypass denial and enable them to develop a process to manage the disagreement in a mature way. Second, it is important that the disagreement should be formulated in words. The different parties need to listen to each other and try to agree on what exactly the disagreement entails. Third, the parties should jointly identify possible strategies to resolve the disagreement and select the strategy the different parties would be most comfortable with. Fourth, when the disagreeing parties are not able to find a way of resolving their disagreement, they need to agree to disagree in a civil and respectful way and decide on guidelines for managing the disagreement in a mature way.

---

2. Langelihle Phakama Malimela, "Analyzing Thabo Mbeki's Policy of 'Quiet Diplomacy' in the Zimbabwean Crisis" (master's thesis, University of Cape Town, 2010).

COMMUNION AS DISAGREEING WELL   43

When the above-mentioned steps do not lead to a satisfactory outcome, the parties need to discern the content of the disagreement and determine if the nature of the disagreement allows any room for just compromises. A just compromise is based on the values of honesty, truth, justice, respect, and fairness for all the parties involved. If a just compromise is not possible, the just cause should not be sacrificed. If quiet diplomacy as a first approach does not lead to a mutually accepted outcome, the justice aspects of the disagreement need to be explicitly stated to make clear the different views in the disagreement. The public stance on a just cause might lead to rejection and accusations in the short term, but time will be on the side of the just cause.

Apartheid was a South African political system that used racial classification as a strategy to discriminate against the majority black population in the country. The white Afrikaner community in South Africa used to be a very religious Christian community. The churches that most Afrikaners were members of developed a theological justification of apartheid. They used the Old Testament story of the Tower of Babel (Gen. 11:1–9) and people speaking in different languages at Pentecost (Acts 2:8–11) as biblical proof that God allows for the differentiation of people. Beyers Naudé, a member of the church, rejected any justification for apartheid and vocalized his disagreement publicly. The Afrikaner community and their churches did not disagree well with Naudé. They did not create opportunities for him to explain the theological motivation for his stand against apartheid. They prejudged him as someone misusing the Bible for political gain and they were too scared to listen to what he had to say. They were afraid that the consequences of his beliefs would lead to the dismantling of white privilege in South Africa. The Afrikaner churches therefore rejected and ostracized Naudé for his public stance against apartheid. The government put him under house arrest for many years and he was not allowed to meet with more than one person at a time. The South African media was not allowed to quote anything he said.

With the fall of apartheid, the democratic South African state embraced Naudé as a national hero for his brave stand against apartheid. The Afrikaner community who had once rejected his position eventually acknowledged that the justification of apartheid was wrong and recognized Naudé as a prophet of his time. The Afrikaner community's journey with Naudé could have been life-giving. They chose to disagree badly. In hindsight, they should have continued listening to him to better understand what he had to say. Instead of walking away, they should have kept walking alongside him. This choice would have meant disagreeing well. It would also have allowed for the possibility of new learning and transformation.

Questions for Reflection

7. For fear of disagreement or conflict, what unjust practices does the Church allow or promote in your context? Why does it do this?
8. What is the most important issue today that the voice of the Church is weak on? How can the prophetic voice of the Church be resourced?

Exercises for Disagreeing Well

On the Emmaus road, in Zimbabwe, and in South Africa there are examples of agreeing badly and examples of agreeing well. In this section, we provide some practical resources for how disagreeing well might be facilitated.

The third way is practiced by first examining your own viewpoint and the case you are putting forward. Then you are asked to put yourself in the other person's shoes as if you are going to defend their side of the story. This, of course, is not easy, as one tends to be so fixed on one's own position. To help you do this, consider the impersonal third person perspective. Imagine your wise grandparent, who sees all sides of the story, who understands fully, who does not take sides, and who offers objective and loving guidance to all involved. This grandparent does not have a personal agenda and has only one objective—a solution that will be for the greater good. Imagine what advice this wise grandparent would give to you. In doing so, it is possible that you will gain a fresh and balanced new appreciation of the situation.

Listening with understanding means listening with attention and without interruptions to the position of the person with whom you disagree. If aspects of the position are not clear, ask questions that will clarify their position.

Do not enter into any form of debate. After listening, share with the person whom you disagree with what you heard the person say. Ask them to correct you if you do not represent their position accurately. If you represented the position accurately, next invite the person to share the feelings they have associated with the position they hold. Reflect back to the person their feelings and ask them to correct you if necessary. In response, ask the person's permission to share your position and feelings in a similar way and invite the person to summarize your position and feelings in their own words. If need be, correct the person where you were not heard accurately.

The counterintuitive way: on the Emmaus road Jesus did the unexpected. To disagree well sometimes requires counterintuitive approaches in the hope that these will facilitate new perspectives and new possibilities. After his release from prison and becoming South Africa's first democratically elected president in 1994, Nelson Mandela, as a gesture of goodwill, invited all the wives of former apartheid era political leaders for tea at his official residence in Pretoria. This was unexpected. Yet through this action, the women's preconceived opinions about Mandela were challenged and they committed to support his reconciliation agenda. Hendrik Verwoerd was the architect of South Africa's apartheid policies. During his leadership as South African prime minister, Mandela was convicted of treason and given a life prison sentence. Betsie, Verwoerd's widow, declined Mandela's invitation and provided as an excuse her frail health. Mandela then traveled more than 600 miles by helicopter to have tea with Betsie Verwoerd in her hometown. She acknowledged she had to adjust her own views about Mandela.

Disagreeing well does not exclude the possibility of conflict. To disagree well requires communicating a difficult message in a way you would like a similar message to be communicated to you. An honest conversation about the reasons for the conflict might require difficult things to be said. Although an honest conversation might hurt initially, the truth will eventually set both parties free.

For many years the international community disagreed with the racist policies of the apartheid South African state. When it became clear that normal diplomacy did not facilitate the required change, the international community decided to impose economic sanctions against South Africa. The economic sanctions more than any other measures eventually contributed to the apartheid government agreeing to relinquish power to a democratically elected government. In hindsight this strategy enabled the disagreement to be resolved in a just way. With the establishment of the democratic South African state in 1994, South Africans who had suffered under the unjust political dispensation expected that their lives would change for the better. When these expectations were not met, the "South Africa must fall" student movement mobilized mass student action in favor of free tertiary education. At the end of 2017, the South African government agreed to the demand of the student movement and announced free tertiary education.

Hearing the Spirit

As has been seen, Jesus created space for disagreement. Such patterns of "space" that are safe enough for disagreeing well remain important today inside and outside the church. In the reconciliation ministry at Coventry Cathedral (UK), the St. Michael's House Protocols are used to help provide spaces for difficult conversations to happen.

Coventry Cathedral was destroyed on the night of November 14, 1940. Provost Howard, looking at the destruction around him after the bombing, took the prophetic and radical decision to not only remember the past but to look forward. Famously, he held two charred pieces of wood from the ruins and said, "Father forgive," acknowledging that we are both victim and perpetrator. Three of the medieval roof nails found in the ruins were bound together into the form of a cross—the cross of nails. The new cathedral was built in 1962 and the cathedral community looked forward with hope to a time of peace and reconciliation. Part of Coventry Cathedral's reconciliation ministry is centered on the Community of the Cross of Nails (CCN). The CCN has three major strands, which further define and explicate what is meant by "disagreeing well." These are spoken of as "healing the wounds of the past," "living with difference and celebrating diversity," and "building a culture of peace."[3]

The St. Michael's House Protocols enable these three strands to be brought into focus when difficult conversations need to happen and to create a safe enough space for "disagreeing well." The protocols are reproduced below.

Protocol One: Respect for the Space

We seek to create a safe enough space where all feel welcome and respected.

We seek to be an inclusive space where all views are heard and diversity is encouraged.

We offer space that is private but not secret.

Protocol Two: Shape the Conversation

We invite participants to give careful attention to each other and therefore:

- Listen actively to those speaking.
- Acknowledge what others say before moving on to have our say.
- Separate people from the problem, the personality from the argument.
- Tell our stories to share about ourselves.

We commit to a process in which we:

- Accept how we and others feel and the legitimacy of our feelings.
- Become mutual and interdependent participants.
- Concern ourselves with shared interests and not defined positions.
- Develop sensitivity to the views and perceptions of others.

We acknowledge our responsibility to:

- Recognize others have a stake in the outcome.
- Remain open to the future we must share.
- Retain our curiosity in the other person.

---

3. "The Community of the Cross of Nails," Coventry Cathedral, accessed August 13, 2019, http://www.coventrycathedral.org.uk/ccn/about-us-2/.

Protocol Three: Share the Learning

We encourage participants, when possible, to openly share knowledge and understanding gained from being part of this space. We expect participants to be free to use any information received, but neither the identity nor affiliation of the speaker, nor that of any other participant, may be revealed. We require that participants refrain from exploiting others with whom they have shared this space by misuse of what has been learnt.[4]

These protocols can be used either in a setting where a difficult conversation needs to take place, or for personal preparation when thinking and praying about such a situation. Prayerfully inviting the Holy Spirit to be present and listening to the Spirit's prompting by slowly reading and absorbing the protocols is one such way to focus on how to disagree well.

Creating a safe enough space to listen to the Spirit and be with "the other" in a disagreement, or equally, as the reconciler between parties, is very important. The St. Michael's House Protocols are one way to create this safe enough space. There are also other things to take into account. The physical space is important: Is it quiet with no interruptions? Is the seating comfortable enough? Are the chairs arranged so everyone can see and be seen (for example, in a circle)? Think about having a focus such as a lit candle in the middle. Offering hospitality helps. Especially when preparing for such a conversation, take the time you need to create both physically and within you a safe enough space to hear the Spirit. Let the Spirit guide you as you prepare, listen, and talk.

As you conclude your reading of this chapter and the reading of scripture, we offer you this closing prayer.

---

4. St. Michael's House Coventry Cathedral, "St. Michael's House Protocols: Guidelines for Seminars and Conversations," November 2011, http://www.shared conversations.org/wp-content/uploads/2015/02/SMH-Protocols.pdf.

A Prayer for Those Who Disagree

Lord, as we try to disagree well,
help us to see that you are in all of us.
As we lament our broken relationships,
help us to risk change and be open to surprise.
As we try to talk together,
help us to hear each other with understanding and compassion.
As we sit at the table,
help us to be courageous enough to stay there with honesty.
As we disbelieve the possibility of change,
help us to be generous and hopeful.
Lord, as we seek a way forward together,
we thank you for walking this journey alongside us.
Amen.

4

Communion as the Hospitality of Disciples

Gloria Mapangdol and Paulo Ueti

Let all guests who arrive be received like Christ,
for He is going to say, "I came as a guest, and you received Me."
(Mt. 25:35)

In the salutation of all guests, whether arriving or departing,
let all humility be shown.
Let the head be bowed
or the whole body prostrated on the ground
in adoration of Christ, who indeed is received in their persons. . . .
Great care and concern are to be shown in receiving poor people and
pilgrims, because in them more particularly Christ is received.
—Rule of Benedict, LIII

This chapter intends to reflect on the importance of hospitality in Christian spirituality. It also tries to challenge our current perspectives and behaviors regarding the "other," the stranger, the one outside our own group, and those who do not share our views. Today the world is marred by intolerance of all sorts (including political and religious fundamentalism) that incites violent behavior and discourse. Given this, and given God's call for God's people to take part in the divine mission toward all creation, it is time for the church to revisit its theology and its spirituality. It is time to get back on track toward the kingdom of God. For we are called to be a parable of the kingdom here and now. We are called to say to the stranger that we are glad to have him/her because he/she is Christ visiting us.[1]

Hearing Scripture

Open Doors, Open Table–Challenge and Inspiration

Hospitality is at the core of the Christian spiritual and theological tradition. It connects and brings "wholyness" to the people and to the environment. The Christian community, the body of Christ, is supposed to be a place for gathering and healing. It is a place to support each other and express to the world that care, mercy, love, and fellowship lead to the practice of justice and the practice of resistance against any kind of violence, inequality, or exclusion. A Christian community is a "hospital." It is a place that offers hospitality, safety, care, and healing where we are to become one, as God is one. Romans 12:13 reminds us all to "contribute to the needs of the saints; extend hospitality."

Part of chapter twelve of Paul's letter to the Romans is a copy from 1 Corinthians 12 that speaks of the community as the risen body of Christ. It is the expression of the living Christ. One distinction we find in Romans 12 is the introduction in verses 1 and 2 that is not present in 1 Corinthians 12:

> I appeal to you therefore, brothers and sisters, by the mercies of God, present your bodies as a living sacrifice, holy and acceptable to God, which is your spiritual worship. Do not be conformed to this world, but be transformed by the renewing of your minds, so that you may discern what is the will of God—what is good and acceptable and perfect.

The community of Christ is a community for change, and the main call to the baptized is to be agents of change. Romans 12:13 starts with the word

---

1. Benedict of Nursia, *The Holy Rule of St. Benedict*, trans. Boniface Verheyen (Grand Rapids, MI: Christian Classics Ethereal Library, 1949), chapter LIII, http://www.documentacatholicaomnia.eu/03d/0480-0547,_Benedictus_Nursinus,_Regola,_EN.pdf.

"communion," which appears as "sharing" in the NIV and the NJB translations, rather than "contribute" as is found in other translations. We all are called to share, to let go, to detach, and to serve others as a way to serve God. The invitation is to share with the "saints." But who are the saints? Too often we think of the "saints" as those who are "without sin, perfect, or irreprehensible." It is good to have in mind that "the saints" are those who decide to accept the call, follow Jesus's way, and dedicate their lives to the kingdom of God.

This invitation to share (ourselves, our resources, our places, our tables) with the saints takes us into a broader invitation from God. We are invited to welcome the vulnerable into our homes—to take care of them, to feed them, and to use our resources for their well-being.[2] After all, being "a stranger" is part of our tradition and faith as Christians. God's people were conscious of their identity as descendant of a "wandering Aramean" welcomed by God (Deut. 26:5–22). This self-reflection becomes the basis for the command to be hospitable toward strangers (Lev. 19:33–34), reflected in various practices, such as those concerning tithing (Deut. 12:17–19) and harvesting (Deut. 24:19–22). The violation of these rules was an offense to God (Judg. 8:4–17).

The theme, invitation, and practice of hospitality in the New Testament is in continuity with the Hebrew Bible.[3] Likewise, the Christian community can be portrayed as immigrants and outsiders/foreigners in a hostile context (1 Pet. 2:11). Therefore, it was part of their identity to "practice hospitality" (Rom. 12:13b), to open their homes to each other (1 Pet. 4:9). The text urges believers to "pursue hospitality." This calling is to a continuous practice. The Greek word here is "to befriend a stranger/foreigner." *Xenia* was a known practice in the Greek culture of the time—the ancient Greek concept of hospitality, which referred to the generosity and courtesy shown to those who were far from home and/or associates of the person bestowing

---

2. See Exod. 22:21; Deut. 10:19; Lev. 19:33–34; Amos 9:7; Isa. 56:1–9; Ps. 146; Ruth 1–4; Matt. 25:31–46; Luke 10:25–37; and John 7:53–8:11.
3. John Koenig, *New Testament Hospitality* (Philadelphia: Fortress Press, 1985), 3.

guest-friendship. The rituals of hospitality created and expressed a reciprocal relationship between guest and host in both material benefits as well as non-material ones.[4]

Luke seemed particularly interested in hospitality, as he alone in his gospel included the stories of the woman who was hospitable (Luke 7:36–50), the good Samaritan (Luke 10:25–37), the prodigal son (Luke 15:11–32), the rich man and Lazarus (Luke 16:19–31), Zacchaeus (Luke 19:1–10), and the Emmaus story (Luke 24:13–35). We will focus on the Emmaus story to demonstrate how hospitality is key in discerning the presence of Christ in the world and following him with boldness and clarity. The destination is certainly important but the way (method, path, and journey) is foundational and fundamental to the process.

This story of two people (a man named Cleopas and perhaps his wife Mary)[5] is often told, retold, played out, read, and reread. In Luke 24:13–35, Cleopas and Mary are running from Jerusalem, getting away from their community, saddened, disappointed. They have lost their hope of liberation because the way they had envisioned it was not the way it actually happened.

We can see in the Gospel of Luke that the community undergoes many difficulties. Good things happened in the years following the unjust arrest, torture, assassination, and resurrection of Jesus. But many doubts and uncertainties grew within the community. New people joined *the Way* (a name given to the early followers of Jesus; see Acts 9:2), including people who did not originally belong to Jesus's tradition and movement: the repressed, the suppressed, and those desperate to be released. These people hoped that someone like King David (male, handsome, influential, rich, powerful, and with the capacity for violence) would come and set them free. They looked for a Messiah who would do all the work. They were not necessarily looking

---

4. Xenia, "Xenia the Ancient Greek Concept of Hospitality," accessed January 31, 2018, http://sfakia-xenia-hotel.gr/en/ancient.

5. According to John 19:25, a man named Cleopas was married to a woman named Mary. For a number of good reasons, it is important to keep the identity of the travelers open. What is not acceptable any longer is to argue that both were definitely men. The word "disciple" is inclusive in its nature.

for a change away from a system that produced oppression. They were looking for their own leader to take the seat of power. They were used to this idea
and they were raised theologically to think that way. However, Jesus chose not
to become this type of Messiah bound by the tradition of King David. Jesus
followed the path of the prophets, including his own cousin John's prophetic
ministry.[6] Jesus was the "suffering servant" or "community messiah" found in
Isaiah 40–56. He was the prophetic Messiah sharing with and defending the
poor and vulnerable.

By our love and desire to serve God, we (the church) welcome the other
because Jesus had "eagerly desired to eat this Passover" with his disciples
before his passion (Luke 22:15). A crucial theological concept—and a key life
experience for believers—is that God always takes the initiative and comes
to meet us, to be with us, to suffer and experience joy with us. He delivers
himself because God is love (1 John 4:19; Hos. 11:1–3). God "will cover you
with his pinions, and under his wings you will find refuge; his faithfulness
is a shield and buckler" (Ps. 91:4). God's gift of himself is unconditional in
a twofold sense. He does not set conditions, nor does he accept constraints.

The idea of the *unconditional gift*, precisely because it is *un*conditional,
runs contrary to human expectations and systems that are exploitative. It is
a challenge to imperialist and capitalist systems. A big part of humanity has
been accustomed to the idea that *truth equals power*. The conditional gift
is understandable to our common sense because it is part of the "normal"
human experience. The unconditional gift/relationship clashes with a worldview dominated by markets that reduce everyone and everything to com-
modities. By this logic, the divine gift must gain recognition. It must establish
itself in history as a powerful triumphant witness. However, this dominant
and domineering thinking confuses the "eyes," and we are prevented from

---

6. It is important to understand that there are two figures of the Messiah in the book
of Isaiah. In the first chapter of Isaiah (1–39, except 24–27), we have the king, the
powerful one, the conqueror, who possesses an army, land, and a palace. But in the
second chapter of Isaiah (40–55), we have the suffering servant. This suffering servant
shaped Jesus's understanding of his messianic path.

recognizing the "real Jesus" (Luke 24:16). Indeed, such thinking has afflicted the development of biblical and theological discourse and even some of our prayer traditions. For example, in the Book of Common Prayer (Brazil), God's mercy may be unconditional, but it is ultimately dependent on human response. God "promises forgiveness to all, *who with sincere penitence and living faith, convert to Him*."[7]

Despite the iniquity that dwells in the heart of humanity since its infancy (Gen. 8:21), God continues to create, because God is love. God himself wants to come close and wants to reveal himself. God's eternal love is unconditional. God comes to us in love, and just as every meeting has the potential for human transformation, so a meeting with divine love transforms our lives. To avoid this encounter through inhospitality is the sin.

Matching the Other's Pace–Approaching Care in the Situation

"How are you?" Have you heard this question today? Did the person who asked you really want your response? Did you respond honestly? This is something to reflect on as we read a portion of the Emmaus story.

> Now on that same day two of them were going to a village called Emmaus, about seven miles from Jerusalem, and talking with each other about all these things that had happened. While they were talking and discussing, Jesus himself came near and went with them, but their eyes were kept from recognizing him. (Luke 24:13–16)

In this story, and in so many others, Jesus matches his pace to theirs and enters deeply into their reality and their rhythm. He wants to continue to be part of their lives. He does not hurry, nor does he invite them to walk according to his pace. He takes on the slow, sad rhythm of these despondent disciples. Jesus was the stranger and the disciples did not recognize him. Their eyes (their perspective, their experience of him and his messianic task) prevented them from recognizing him.

---

7. Igreja Episcopal Anglicana do Brasil, *Livro de Oração Comum* (Porto Alegre: Livraria Anglicana, 9ª Edição, 2009), 29, emphasis added.

Questions for Reflection

1. When a "stranger" approaches, what do we do? Do we listen? Do we learn from him/her?
2. There is a spiritual request here to approach, to make yourself close to strangers, foreigners, and people in need and in pain. How might this be achieved in your context?

"What are you discussing with each other while you walk along?" (Luke 24:17). Jesus is interested in engaging with these people and their lives. He wants to weave himself into the fabric of their lives (text, body, spoken words, feelings). Meeting people and enabling them to participate in the life of the community or family is a requirement in following the way of Jesus. Yet this attitude of Jesus seems strange in Luke's text. Jesus knows firsthand what has happened. Why is he asking them this question? Is it a test? They think that Jesus, a stranger, should have known what had happened. But Jesus's question—his intervention—is to invite them into his life again: the real life, not the one imagined by them. He leads them to articulate and to analyze the facts from their own point of view, including their hopes and especially their disappointments. He wants to help the two travelers to revisit their lives and the interpretations of their lives and the scriptures, in order to experience the love of God's kingdom, the dream of transformation and of happiness.

Welcoming, Respecting, Listening

In Judeo-Christian spirituality, hospitality is fundamental, both in the face of the divine and of the "other" who inhabits the world we live in. Jesus's question about the disciples' conversation on the road elicits a reaction. They appear horrified or deeply curious, even offended at the stranger's ignorance. Again, it is interesting to consider the question of why he asked something so apparently obvious. Given the testimony of Jesus, welcoming strangers is a divine act. Indeed, God's act of creation is a divine act of welcome. We are visitors and stewards on the planet we live on. It is given to us by God as an act of pure love. In sharing space and engaging in conversation, we carry knowledge, feelings, skills, experiences, and curiosity.

Jesus's action allowed the disciples to revisit their experience and tell it in their own words. Jesus invited them into an emerging therapeutic and educational process.

Accompaniment and words heal and transform all involved. This is why Jesus does not at first explain his own understanding of events. When we offer (like Jesus did throughout his life) ourselves, our perspectives, words, and places for others, we offer the possibility of healing and building up our growing community. The Christian community is called to be a safe space for all. It is a "hospital" to heal and welcome those in need and those in pain. People living in poverty, in vulnerability and suffering, need a guaranteed and respected space of physical safety in which they can speak and be heard, in which their voice is accorded its full value and validity.

In the Emmaus story, the disciples, as people disillusioned and without hope, are in the process of disconnecting from their community. Their idea of the Messiah is ultimately unfulfilled by Jesus the outcast, visitor, and stranger who remains in need of a place to stay. Their encounter, however, with this suffering Messiah produced life, energy, recognition, and courage to regain purpose and rejoin the community transformed and empowered.

Which Texts, Which Theology?

While still on the road—unlearning and learning—Jesus, the stranger, invited these travelers into a "conversa(c)tion." He said nothing new. Rather, he pointed them to a new way of looking at scriptural texts and a new way of understanding their lives and assumptions. Jesus took up the disciples' story and interpreted it in a way they did not expect. Imprisoned as they were by a theology complicit with empire and religious comfort, Jesus offered them a new perspective on the nature and mission of the Messiah. He started with the things they already knew but had forgotten, or had been "prevented from understanding" by the dominant way of thinking. They had been waiting for someone to solve their problem. Many people were formed in this passive expectation that someone more powerful, more educated, more mature, and more experienced would lead them and solve their problems. That person was not Jesus.

A theology of the Messiah as king who resolves everything (for a certain group) exists in the prophets (see Isa. 1–39). But there is, as we have seen, another image and theology of the Messiah as suffering servant (see Isa. 40–55). Jesus's disciples—and especially those identified as the twelve—are depicted as lacking this insight. All the teaching about the cross in the foretelling of the Passion (Mark 8:31–10:45) leads to discord between Jesus and the disciples on the question of his Messiahship. Here, it is not simply a question of reading, studying, and interpreting scripture, but of asking: Which interpretation should we take, to what end, using which texts? Is the Good News of Jesus for everyone?

Hospitality—A Requirement to Follow God's Will

They were awaiting the king Messiah, "the one to redeem Israel" (Luke 24:21). The two traveling to Emmaus expected a king like David, or a liberator like Moses, who would physically confront those in power by violent means and take their place. They had not realized that these two figures, having freed the people and taken power, were corrupted by that same power and ended up shaping and exercising their power in ways similar to the pharaohs. A look at the texts is enough to confirm that David and Moses were not good leadership models to follow. Toward the end of their lives, both became violent, overbearing, and corrupt. Any institution run by a sole individual runs this risk.

The disciples' image of the Messiah and the redemption of Israel did not fit with Jesus and his way of redeeming suffering and exploited lives. This is why their eyes were "prevented" from recognizing Jesus as he walked with them. Their Jesus was the one walking at their side, but they could not recognize him because they did not expect him. Jesus's call to action and his rereading of the biblical texts was intended to help them see with new eyes. Later, they would testify, "Were not our hearts burning within us while he was talking with us on the road, while he was opening the scriptures to us?" (Luke 24:32).

The disciples invited the "stranger" to their house, to safety and for food and company during the dangerous period of the night. This action changed everything. By gathering as community, by welcoming all to the table, by sharing life and stories, by spending time listening to each other and having a meal together, their eyes were opened. The importance of rereading the scriptures was recognized, and they recovered their courage and desire to get back to building up the messianic community again.

Always Moving Forward

We will closely study Jesus's actions, which must be our light and our model as we engage with people today. Reading the Bible means also, as Jesus did, reading our everyday lives alert always to context and the changes within context. Jesus first approaches the couple on the road, taking the initiative. He is welcomed by the travelers with kindness. He initiates the first step. God always comes to meet us. God is unconditional and constant love. Jesus's second action is to walk together with the other two. Through relationship the strangeness and assumptions are reframed. His third action is to ask about their lives—he asks them what is going on and what is making them sad. Following Jesus, we are invited to share our lives. We are invited to listen with respect, interest, and open minds to learn from others. God is speaking through this. Scriptural knowledge is not enough to see Jesus. Action is needed to open our eyes and change our perspectives and realities. Jesus says, "You give them something to eat yourselves" (Matt. 14:16). You, get involved. You, do something.

Questions for Reflection

3. How can we turn the sadness, the impulse to flee, the fear, and the inability to recognize Jesus at the start of the walk to Emmaus into an Easter pilgrimage? How do we make it to the eucharistic table?
4. What does it mean to realize that the way to resurrection is not to flee but to return to Jerusalem (to the conflicts, to the cross, to our everyday life)?

The Emmaus road disciples regained hope and courage to return to Jerusalem. They returned to the conflicts and to the crises. They returned to rebuild another possible world full of new relationships. Their dark night now became the dawn of resurrection. "Even the darkness is not dark to you; the night is as bright as the day, for darkness is as light to you" (Ps. 139:12).

Hearing Each Other

Hospitality as a Means to Break Down Barriers and Address Social Issues

A seminarian was hosted by a poor family for her fieldwork. The family prepared the best food for her to eat and the best part of the house for her to sleep in. As a result, some of the members of the family were sleeping on the floor. In addition, she found out that the special food prepared for her was bought through credit from a nearby store. If she did not accept this kind of hospitality, the family would be hurt and discouraged. We do not encourage this kind of hospitality, but we have to accept it graciously and perhaps introduce changes later. This experience was humbling on the part of the seminarian. As a result, she bought food and shared it with the family. In the course of their sharing, the family came to realize that as part of the family she would eat what they ate and she would sleep where they slept.

In most cases, the hospitality of the poor and marginalized is more remarkable than that of the rich. The rich can often give away huge sums of money. Sometimes these amounts are quite insignificant to them. Unlike the poor, however, the rich do not dare welcome strangers into their homes. The poor, on the other hand, may think they have little to offer, but are still willing to welcome those who are weary and hungry into their homes. Often the poor would do everything to respond to the needs of others, even to the point of adding a burden unto themselves. There is a huge difference in these two kinds of hospitality. One is afraid of the risk whilst giving money. The other takes the risk and does his/her best with little or no money.

In many communities, the rich build high walls separating themselves from the rest of the community. Walls divide. Walls can be physical, but they can also be personal, social, economic, or political. These walls come together with issues of injustice, animosity, indifference, and discrimination.

They need to be broken down for true hospitality to take place. Sometimes those who build walls hold on to the false hope of enjoying their privacy and protection against those around them. However, walls are detrimental to relationships, peace, and reconciliation. We can identify many examples of this. In contrast, when people are given opportunities to meet each other, talk, share stories, listen, and interact, understanding takes place and often leads to transformation. With walls, these hopes for peace and reconciliation are never realized. Jesus started as a stranger to the two Emmaus disciples, but after their encounter and fellowship, he was a stranger no more. As the letter to the Ephesians says, "For he is our peace; in his flesh he has made both groups into one and has broken down the dividing wall, that is, the hostility between us . . . that he might create in himself one new humanity in place of the two, thus making peace, and might reconcile both groups to God in one body through the cross" (Eph. 2:14–16).

Even the most powerful and educated can still learn from the poorest or marginalized in the community if they are open to listening and learning. Sometimes one can be surprised to learn new and important things at an unexpected time, in an unexpected place, or from an unexpected person.

Questions for Reflection

5. Who are the poor and marginalized in our communities?
6. How do we extend hospitality to the poor and marginalized (these may include the socioeconomically poor, victims of war and injustices, refugees, women, LGBTQ, or others)?

Abused Women Welcomed by Church Hospitality

Brazil is ranked fifth in the world in regard to the domestic violence crime index. There are about thirteen femicides per day in the country. Most of these murders are perpetrated by family members or acquaintances of the victim. Only a small percentage get any police attention. The church, as the body of Christ, is a community that is called to become a "spiritual house" (1 Pet. 2:5) to welcome the vulnerable. We must remain mindful that whatever we do to Jesus's sisters and brothers, we do to Jesus himself.

In 2010, the Holy Trinity Parish in the northern part of the Province of Brazil decided to do something about the cries of abused women and children. The church accepted the challenge from the municipality to offer a safe space to shelter them. Prior to this, there was no space provided in the whole region to host these women. It was an urgent need, and the parish knew that the church sees Christ abused in those abused women and children. The safe space has been established as the Noeli House and continues to operate today with the support and participation of the whole Christian community. Currently the Noeli House hosts women for a period of up to 3 months, with spaces for approximately 140 women and 200 children at one time. The women's police department files the reports from these women and the house offers psychological, pedagogical, pastoral, medical, legal, and social assistance, along with training to help them become more financially independent.

Learning from Luke's community teaching, the Holy Trinity Parish took the initiative to approach those women and children. It decided to walk with them, closely and with care. The community is a space for listening and healing. The body of Christ (the Church) acts as a safe place to be, to grow, to evolve, and to inspire and challenge others.

Questions for Reflection

7. To whom do you make yourself a "neighbor"? With whom will you walk?
8. To what extent is the Christian community you belong to a place for healing and listening? How might it listen better and bring more healing?
9. How might our liturgy (public service) serve the most vulnerable?

Hospitality and Communion in the Church

Today we still hear of many churches, including some Anglican churches, who close their doors and exclude certain groups of people. What does this imply about the life and work of the church? The signage you see in every Episcopal church in the Philippines carries these words: "The Episcopal/Anglican Church Welcomes You." You surely have your own "welcome" signs in your own churches. Yet how serious are we when we say that we welcome people? Do we welcome them only in order to fill up the pews? Do we welcome them hoping to get something in return? Do we consider them as part of the family and involve them in the life of the church?

Aside from the controversial issue of LGBTQ people in the church, there is also the issue of welcoming refugees and migrants in one's church or community. In many places, the issue of racial discrimination still exists. How does the church fulfill its mission of welcoming in God's people if barriers are set even before the doors of the churches are opened? What is keeping us from embracing people who are different from us? If Jesus gave chances to those who were discouraged, hopeless, and weak, does the church not find it important to give hope to the hopeless and voice to those silenced? Hospitality is integral to our life as Christians. It is not something we should do occasionally but is a given character of the church. Christine Pohl is right when she argues that hospitality is a way of life and never a means to an end. If hospitality is used as a strategy for church evangelism or church growth, it is manipulative and will not be sustained.[8]

Jesus did not use his position to manipulate his followers. On the road to Emmaus he initiated the conversation, then listened intently before responding to the needs of these despondent disciples. Shall we then wait on people to approach the doorsteps of the church or should we be true to God's mission (the *missio Dei*)? God's mission is not stagnant but moving and exploring new possibilities. If we are to become agents of change, it has to come from the inside and be shared with others as well. We cannot distance ourselves from what is happening in the society and in the world. We need always to widen our horizons and respond to the needs of others beyond the church.

When we share the Holy Eucharist together, we are reminded of a ministry of servanthood, exemplified by the Son of God who gave his life for us. Why then would we deny this fellowship to others? Robert Karris contends that the Emmaus table fellowship "reveals a God who wants to sit down at table with everyone and will remove all obstacles, even that of death, which

---

8. Christine D. Pohl, "The Healthy Church: Embodying Hospitality," *Catalyst*, February 1, 2003, http://www.catalystresources.org/the-healthy-church-embodying -hospitality.

stand in the way of the accomplishment of that communion."[9] Should not we as a church participate in the removal of obstacles rather than be those who stand in the way of such communion?

In many contexts, the poor, the marginalized, strangers, and those who suffer come to church as a last resort. They may have been ignored or deprived by their families or by their own communities, and they look to our churches as their last hope. If our doors are also closed, we may well be guilty of extinguishing the last spark of hope in their lives. The Emmaus story clearly shows Jesus approaching with care the disciples who turned away from Jerusalem and who had lost hope because of the death of their master. At his initiative, they regained hope and were transformed to be better servants of the master. Can we not as a church follow what the master did too? Karris reminds us, "God's kingly conquest of sin and death . . . comes from opening oneself to the unwanted and unexpected dimensions of Christian discipleship and by extending welcoming hands to strangers."[10]

Questions for Reflection

10. How do the churches in your context define and practice the word "welcome"?
11. To what extent do you think the Church has become more exclusive today than in New Testament times? Why is this the case?
12. What does the Church need to give up in order to fully practice hospitality?

Hearing the Spirit

We are born in connection, we are wounded through disconnection, and we are healed through reconnection.

—Hedy Schleifer (therapist)

9. Cited by Arthur Just in *An Ongoing Feast* (Collegeville, MN: Liturgical Press, 1993), 254.
10. Robert J. Karris, *Eating Your Way Through Luke's Gospel* (Collegeville, MN: Liturgical Press, 2006), 50.

Combining Meditation with Contemplation: A Spiritual Exercise

In our histories, and in the ways we read the Bible, there is movement and there are processes of transformation in all levels of life. This starts with the "desire to get moving" and to enter into the universe of the other. Here there is a desire to be accepted and welcomed as you are, and to participate in another's life. This desire means not letting the connection drop and not permitting disconnection to set in. Jesus the "visitor" and the "stranger" took the initiative and drew near. Jesus made himself close (a neighbor) to the people.

Jesus's spirit-filled initiative is our example. Because of the power of the Spirit at work in his life, we are called to discernment and contemplation as part of mission. That is to say, a first step to becoming a neighbor is found in meditation. There is a great tradition of such meditation in Christian history. Sometimes it takes time to think of something in order to begin one's meditation. Meditating quietly in a pleasant place away from noise and any kind of distraction is the easiest way for many people. Equally, meditation can be done out in the streets by sitting and observing people as they pass by. As you watch, ask yourself, who are these people? What do they do? Why do they walk and act in this or that way? Imagine, then, that you are Jesus and you are walking with them—what would you tell them? Would they bother to look at you? Would they welcome you to join their journey? Would there be a difference in how the poor and the rich treat you? Reflect on these things as you observe the people. After pondering on each question, spend some time in prayer for the people. Pray especially for God's guidance in whatever circumstances these people are in and whichever part of the journey they are on with Jesus. Pray that at some point, they would welcome Jesus to dine with them. In this way, the act of sitting in a coffee shop can be transformed. Instead of surfing the net or focusing on the self, the heart is opened to the very ministry of Jesus's hospitality in our everyday lives.

Immersion as Meditation: A Spiritual Exercise

In the Philippine context, you cannot really understand what is happening without immersing yourself in the situation. Many people who have not experienced hardship or poverty in their own lives cannot fully understand what it is like to live this way. Coming down from your own pedestal and having fellowship with people who are struggling will teach you much and even strengthen your own spirituality. Try being in their shoes even for a short while. Try eating what they eat and doing what they do. Listen to their stories. In many cases, you will be surprised to find that most poor people, no matter the hardship, count their blessings more than their hardships. Immersion often leads to realization. You discover facts concerning the situation itself or something about your own weaknesses and strengths. Ultimately, understanding the reality can lead you to be more focused on action and prayer. Knowing the real needs and struggles, you can express your prayers more specifically than those formulated at a distance.

Reading the Bible Contextually: A Spiritual Exercise

We must forge ways to avoid perceiving the stranger/visitor as a disease to be eradicated, or a danger to be avoided. Hospitality finally opened the eyes of the travelers to Emmaus. Here, "opened eyes" is a metaphor for understanding and practicing the faith. The clear intention is to collaborate in order to create a space of hospitality, solidarity, and recommitment on the way to God's reconciling mission for all of creation. Consequently, one of the final questions of any Bible study should always be, what does this study (this journey of ours with Jesus) compel us to do?

It is always a challenge to take the study of the biblical texts seriously. Yet reading the scriptures is a great opportunity to hear what the Holy Spirit is telling us. The "Contextual Bible Study Methodology" offers a path for communities to hear the Spirit in their Christian formation. Reading the Bible opens us all to the stranger, to the love of each other, and to the suspension of prejudice. Like the story of Emmaus, there are steps on this journey of biblical discovery.

- Start with a prayer or liturgy to set the ambience and to give thanks to God for the gathering. Ask God to transform you in the reading and the studying of his Word.

- Approach those in need. Take the initiative to understand where people's needs are. Mission—moving out of our comfort zone—is a requirement of being a disciple.
- Match the pace of the community. Pay attention to the community's reality. Join their context and walk in their rhythm, being careful not to trespass. Try to become acquainted. Be a friend. Show a desire to journey together. Company is paramount on the journey. Be curious and respectful.
- Show interest in the local context. When churches establish programs of training for discipleship, the first questions should be "What is going on?" and "What are you discussing as you walk along?" (Luke 24:17) Being part of our Anglican Communion is very helpful in exchanging experiences and information to foster deeper and lasting disciples for the kingdom of God.
- Be ready to be silent and to listen. The voice of the people and their reality are important. Discipleship requires silence on the part of one in order to listen to the other deeply and in loving care. Integrate spaces for mutual listening and dialogue. This is a good way to listen to what God is revealing through his children. Transformation, peace, and reconciliation are achieved through true processes of silence, dialogue, and mutual listening.
- Read the Bible together and engage in study for transformation. How can you see the presence of Jesus reinterpreting your reality? How do you see Jesus in the "little ones," in the "others," in suffering?
- Practice hospitality. Be welcoming and establish safe and welcoming places. This is an essential part of Christian spirituality. Open your hearts, your churches, and your thoughts. The clear intention of sharing (understanding in deeper ways, analyzing contextual realities, reading the Bible together, and sharing the table) is to build communities of collaboration. These communities create spaces of hospitality, solidarity, and commitment to life, to "the way," and to all creatures and creation.

- Bless (say and undertake good words/actions) and stay in communion despite the tensions. The Eucharist reminds us that justice, peace, and reconciliation have been achieved *and* are yet to be achieved. Living in the "in-between time" is to live with each other even in disagreement. To witness to God's way, we need good words and actions (they themselves are blessings) and we must share our lives and resources to strengthen our hearts for the journey.

Hospitality is crucial to the spirituality of many religions and a command to the people of God. Let us pay attention to what happens when you, for instance, spend time with refugees, listen to their stories, hold their hands, and, most importantly, look into their eyes. When hospitality is not provided, bad things happen (Gen. 18–19). A vast range of Bible studies confirm this. The disciples of Emmaus did what their faith compelled them to do. They invited the stranger into their home. They shared their house, their hearts, and their food. Welcoming and being intentionally close to a stranger is a bold action. When we have the courage to do it, marvelous things can happen. It is amazing to discover what we can learn from them and amazing to discover what we have to share.

Do not underestimate the power of hospitality. We share our contexts, we read the Bible in community, and we worship together. Here are signs of discipleship. We are known as disciples and we become disciples by following Jesus, loving one another, sharing resources, and being faithful stewards of creation.

5

Communion as Disciplined Sharing

Janice Price and John Kapya Kaoma

In the Anglican Communion, one key way of sharing in the gospel is expressed through diocesan companion links from the South to the South and from the South to the North. Friendships between parishes, through Anglican agencies and other mission agencies, and informal relationships all express the variety of connections that bring sharing to life. These relationships exist to further the mission of God in the world. As God's people, we share Christ with each other. In this regard, disciplined sharing includes receiving Christians from other parts of the world. The growing number of non-Western Christians in the global North invites humility to receive the gift of Christ afresh across cultural differences. Their presence is another act of sharing the faith. Importantly, the resources God calls the church to share are ourselves, our lives, our challenges, our joys and sorrows—all expressed through friendship in Christ, of which gift-giving is an important part.

What is disciplined sharing? Readers may be surprised to see the association of the words "disciplined" and "sharing." Disciplined sharing is about being part of the Anglican Communion and working within its structures. Though not the only way, these structures enable both formal and informal relationships. Many companion links have a formal agreement that exists between dioceses. It is the discipline of a structure that allows relationships to flourish within a common understanding. Paul set up a structure for disciplined sharing through a network of churches in what has become known as the "Jerusalem collection" (2 Cor. 8–9). Our structures and networks do the same thing.

Sharing is at the heart of Christian life. The scriptures encourage and urge Christians to be generous, kind, and willing to share who they are as well as the resources God has given to the church (Heb. 13:1–3). Our sharing is a response to God's generosity to us in Jesus Christ. As the grand giver, God invites us to share divine blessings with each other. For the earliest Christians, for example, sharing was a way of life (Acts 2:44–47). This model has characterized the church throughout the generations. Indeed, central to our assemblies is a sharing in the Eucharist, which itself reminds us of God's self-sharing love for humanity. But it also reminds us of our responsibility to share God's love with one another. As Paul argues, Christ "emptied himself," and thus, we are called to look to the interests of others (Phil. 2:4–7).

There are many factors that inhibit Christian sharing. The history of colonialism, neocolonialism, global economic inequalities, and theological differences can present insurmountable barriers to sharing across cultures. But living out communion invites Christians to relate with each other with the loving eyes of God. In short, sharing is a spiritual discipline through which Christians encounter the triune God revealed in the self-giving life of Jesus Christ. In this chapter, we employ Paul's practice of sharing and other examples of sharing in the Anglican Communion as examples of disciplined sharing.

Hearing Scripture

Paul and the Jerusalem Collection

It is easy to miss the Jerusalem collection in Paul's letters. However, it is one of the most important threads running through his letters and appears at various points, most notably in 2 Corinthians 8 and 9.

The church in Jerusalem was suffering great hardship as the result of a famine. Paul became aware of this situation through meeting with Peter, James, and John, the leaders of the Jerusalem church (Gal. 2:10). While visiting the various churches in his apostolic role, Paul encouraged them to give generously for the needs in Jerusalem. Paul urges the Corinthians to finish their work for the collection so that it can be taken to Jerusalem (2 Cor. 8:11). In this passage Paul is expressing his theology and practice of giving.

Jesus Christ–The Model for All Giving (2 Cor. 8:8-10)

Paul describes the Incarnation as Christ voluntarily and willingly giving up the riches of his heavenly life to come to earth for the salvation of God's creation. In Paul's way of expressing the Incarnation, in 2 Corinthians 8:9, he describes it as a divine gift or exchange. The pattern is Christ. He gave up riches and willingly embraced poverty in order that humanity might come to know the riches of God's grace on this earth and for eternity. From this point, the lives of all believers and of Christ's church are to express and embody the life-giving divine exchange.

Paul is appealing to the faith of the Corinthians to complete their contribution to their brothers and sisters in Jerusalem. He does not command them to give but urges and encourages them to be generous and follow the example of the Macedonian churches. Paul is testing the sincerity of their love (2 Cor. 8:8). He knows that to command the Corinthians will not get him very far. Although the text does not give the details, there had been tension and misunderstandings between them and Paul; it is likely that a group in the church wanted to pull away from Paul's apostolic authority and from the collection that Paul espoused. Paul accurately judges the mood of the church in appealing to its higher calling in Christ.

The city of Corinth was a busy international port. It was socially, religiously, and economically diverse. This socioeconomic diversity was evident in a church where it was likely that both slaves and Roman citizens were part of the faith community (1 Cor. 7:20–24). Social relationships were challenging but provided a great opportunity to witness to the power of transformed relationships in Christ. In 2 Corinthians, Paul is urging reconciliation between the church and himself as well as between church members. Here he speaks from his heart more than in any other letter. He encourages them to show and practice a sincerity of love through completing their contribution to the Jerusalem collection. They began with such enthusiasm and zeal. Now they must demonstrate they understand the meaning of God's gift by blessing others through their generosity. For in such generosity they too shall be blessed (Acts 20:35).

Building Relationships in the Body of Christ

What was the purpose of the collection for the believers in Jerusalem? Paul committed himself to mobilizing resources among his churches because of the extreme hardship and famine some were experiencing. But it was not only about their material needs. The collection had another purpose. At the end of his letter to the Romans, Paul writes, "For if the Gentiles have come to share in their spiritual blessings, they ought also to be of service to them in material things" (Rom. 15:27). Paul ministered on the edge of one of the biggest divides in the ancient world—the divide between Jews and Gentiles. The Jews believed in one God, and the Greco-Roman world was dominated by the worship of many gods. Many Jews lived outside Jerusalem in diaspora communities under Roman rule but managed to worship in their own way within it.

Paul and the churches he founded challenged this divide. The churches brought together Jews and Gentiles who were all followers of Jesus. Churches were particularly appealing to God-fearers who were Gentiles attracted to the Jewish way of worship. The church in Corinth included people from different social classes—Roman citizens, migrants, and slaves. The message of Paul is that these earthly divisions were immaterial. What matters is our unity in Christ (Gal. 3:28). As Rowan Williams writes, "Belonging to God's people is being neither a Jew nor a Gentile; it's a third reality beyond the rival identities of different sorts of insider—the 'insideness' of the Jew confident in God's choice of Israel, the 'insideness' of the Roman citizen."[1]

To look to the Anglican Communion, the generosity of churches breaks down earthly barriers. Bishop Charles Mackenzie (1825–1862) fought

---

1. Rowan Williams, *Meeting God in Paul: Reflections for the Season of Lent* (London: SPCK Publishing, 2015), 32.

against slavery and colonialism. Archbishop Janani Luwum (1922–1977) fought against Idi Amin. Archbishop Desmond Tutu (b. 1931) has fought against apartheid and ongoing injustice. Each of these examples speaks to the role the Anglican Communion has played and continues to play in the world. Anglican provinces and dioceses continue to be involved in generous practices of reconciliation in places such as Israel and Palestine, Sudan and South Sudan, and India and Pakistan. Then there are the countless smaller reconciliations that the church enables, though they never hit the headlines. The struggle against malaria and HIV/AIDS and the mission for education are among the many acts of generosity in which the Communion is involved.

Paul was the right person for this ministry on the edge. He embodied both Jewish heritage and, as a Roman citizen, imperial privilege. What defined him was being a follower of Jesus Christ (Phil. 3:4–8). The Jerusalem collection was, in Paul's vision, an instrument of unity between Jewish and Gentile believers. In expressing practical concern for the Jerusalem followers of Jesus, Paul hoped that old divisions would be overcome. He hoped for the believers to connect with each other in new ways. This was a risky venture. Paul was not sure whether the Gentile Christians would contribute and whether the Jewish followers of Jesus would accept such a gift from Gentiles. He argues in his letter to the Romans that as the Gentiles have received spiritual blessings from the Jews, in the person of Jesus, so the Gentiles will want to share their material blessings with the followers of Jesus in Jerusalem.

The Jerusalem collection is much more than a material gift. It is a spiritual blessing among believers reflecting the gift of Jesus to them. The goal is fellowship and equality (2 Cor. 8:14). Although the emphasis is on the giver, receiving the gift demands humility. Paul appeals to Gentile Christians whose spiritual identity is dependent upon Jewish witness.[2] The Jewish community must be humble enough to receive the gifts from their Christian brothers and sisters—most of whom they had never seen or met. This giving can be a

---

2. Tom Wright, *Paul: A Biography* (London: SPCK Publishing, 2018), 340.

reminder to all of us—we need to give as well as to receive material blessings from each other.

The giver should have little cause for pride in the giving. Income inequalities are results of the capitalist global order that takes advantage of global South countries. The riches of Europe, North America, and some Asian countries are propelled by capitalism—and Christian churches benefit from it. To rewrite Paul's words, the Westerners have received global South natural goods for centuries, so they owe it to global South nations to share with them their material blessings. Such sharing does not exclude fighting the injustices that feed the inequalities. As Archbishop William Temple argued, injustice is not addressed by charity but only by justice.[3]

Generosity

Generosity is at the heart of Christian living. It was for Paul and it is for Christians today. The Anglican Communion aspires to be a generous community of churches united in their Anglican identity for the sake of God's mission in the world. While the Corinthian church was materially prosperous, something had happened to interrupt their contribution to the collection. It is not known what interrupted their giving, but Paul rejoices when Titus brings him the news of repentance among the Corinthians. From this rejoicing, in 2 Corinthians 8, he goes immediately into urging them to continue to give.

Paul knew about the problem. Rather than ignoring it, as a teacher and pastor he does not command the Corinthians to give but encourages them to do so. He uses the example of the generosity of the Macedonian churches (Philippi, Thessalonica, and Berea) to urge the Corinthians to do their best in providing aid to those in need. The churches in Macedonia had been undergoing persecution. The followers of Jesus in Philippi had experienced persecution following Paul's disruption of the business community through his casting out the demon from the young girl who was a fortune-teller (Acts

---

3. William Temple, *Christianity and Social Order* (New York: Penguin Books, 1942), 14–15.

16:16–24). While Paul moved on to Thessalonica, the effects were still felt by the church. Yet during poverty, hardship, and persecution, the Philippian church gave generously for their brothers and sisters in Jerusalem. Paul writes to the Corinthians that the Macedonian churches, even during persecution, gave generously (2 Cor. 8:1–5). Generosity creates generosity. Sharing encourages sharing.

The Macedonian churches' attitude toward sharing may speak to another aspect of disciplined sharing. It is not the economic situation that determines Christian sharing—the needs do. As disaster after disaster hits the world, one wonders whether, for example, churches in Africa should consider contributing to rebuilding efforts beyond the continent. Efforts of sharing animals and grain with Christians in the global North and beyond may need to be revisited—we all have a responsibility to give and to receive. Rather than ignoring this Christian gesture of sharing, resources may be sold and the money given for the relief of others. Sharing demands humility. It is important that churches in the global North learn to receive as well as give.

Transparency

Titus was Paul's coworker and partner in the gospel. He was important to Paul's ministry with the Corinthians, acting as a go-between or mediator. Paul considers him to be trustworthy, and Titus goes to Corinth on his own initiative to take the letter and receive the collection. He was Greek and had first worked with Paul at the church in Antioch. He accompanied Paul on his visit to Jerusalem to take an earlier gift from the church in Antioch to the believers in Jerusalem. He became the subject of some controversy, even a test case, about his status as an uncircumcised follower of Jesus. Paul and Barnabas argued that he did not need to be circumcised because following Jesus was enough (Acts 15). This approach became the norm for Gentile believers.

It is determined that Titus will receive the Corinthian contribution to the collection together with an unnamed brother and will take it to Paul (2 Cor. 8:18). Then a larger group, representing the contributing churches, will take the collection to Jerusalem. At every point Paul is careful to be transparent and accountable for the transmission of the money. A large group is commissioned with the task. There is safety in numbers as well as mutual accountability. These representatives had to be people who could carry the responsibility of taking the gift to Jerusalem. There were no easy ways of moving money. It was not a simple task. They were carrying a large amount of money across land and sea, where they could be subject to violence. They had courage for the sake of the gospel.

The account of the Jerusalem collection is relevant for the church today. Paul was concerned to link the identity of the churches he founded and to help them to see themselves as part of the same ministry of proclaiming Jesus to the world. They had a shared identity as followers of Jesus and he wanted them to know this in their life together. The resources they shared were their faith in Christ and their friendship in the gospel. The financial gift expressed this fellowship: "If one member suffers, all suffer together with it; if one member is honored, all rejoice together with it" (1 Cor. 12:26).

Questions for Reflection

1. Where do you see the expression of the "divine exchange" in your life and in your church?
2. What examples of generosity have inspired you? What effect did they have on your practice of giving?
3. How would you describe attitudes to giving in your church? Are they like the Corinthian or the Macedonian churches?
4. How do you ensure transparency in your practices of giving and receiving?

Sharing as Ubuntu

The African concept of *ubuntu* also speaks to this model of biblical disciplined sharing. From this perspective, humanity cannot exist in isolation from each other—we are social beings. The maxims *umuntu ngubuntu ngabantu* in Xhosa, *munhu nekuda kwevanhu,* and the Sotho *motho ke motho ka batho* all translate as "a person is a person through other persons." The Bemba of Zambia also say *icalo bantu* (the world is people), pointing again to how human existence is dependent on disciplined sharing. In short, all these maxims express how the Bantu understand life in community—we belong together. In fact, "we can tell when *ubuntu* is there and when it is absent. It has to do with what it means to be truly human, to know that you are bound up with others in the bundle of life."[4]

In Bantu communities, sharing is a virtue. It is expected of every human being to share what he or she has with those without. Solidarity with others is an important virtue. If one kills an animal for meat, one is expected to share with other members of the village. As it is said, *akacepa kakufwala, icakulya ta cicepa* (cloth sizes can be small, but not the food). Moreover, a person who does not share is said to be *umupondo* (an enemy of the community). Children are repeatedly told to share anything they have with their friends. A child who refuses to share is negatively perceived. Similarly, when a member of the village dies, members are not only obliged to attend the funeral, but also to contribute to the food as well as to the burial of the deceased. In short, sharing is another way in which we express our love and solidarity with one another. It speaks to the biblical command to love one's neighbor as oneself (Mark 12:28–34).

The value of *ubuntu* is that it is a conceptual tool to hold ourselves accountable to each other. We are one earth community. As humans, we have rights and responsibilities. Chief among our responsibilities is sharing. As former South African president Thabo Mbeki writes, the world "is an interdependent whole in which none can be truly free unless all are free, in which none can be truly prosperous unless none elsewhere in the world goes hungry, and in which none of us can be guaranteed a good quality of life unless we act together to protect the environment."[5]

Desmond Tutu also writes:

[T]o share prosperity of affluent countries with indigent ones is not really altruism. It is ultimately the best kind of self-interest, for if the

---

4. Desmond Tutu, *God Has a Dream: A Vision of Hope for Our Time* (New York: Doubleday, 2004), 27, and *No Future Without Forgiveness* (New York: Doubleday, 1999), 26.
5. Thabo Mbeki, "The African Renaissance, South Africa and the World," United Nations University, April 9, 1998, http://www.unu.edu/unupress/mbeki.html.

poor countries become prosperous in their turn, then they provide vigorous markets for the consumer goods produced elsewhere. The debt burden is a bomb that could shatter the economy of the globe to smithereens. And so a new and just economic order would benefit both the rich and poor nations.[6]

Despite the challenges in which the Church in Africa exists, communalism—that is, sharing—is a virtue. The moral virtues of sharing, solidarity, and interdependence are all elements of *ubuntu*.[7] It is key to cross-cultural expressions of sharing. Sharing cannot exist without solidarity, caring, love, and sympathy. These values are not unique to African cultures but can relate to other social relationships. For Christians, God is *ubuntu*. God loves, God cares, and God is always in solidarity with those in need. Thus, the values of *ubuntu* are universal and have deep theological significance. Since life is shared, Africans may expect global North Christians to share their resources with them. Unlike in the global North, where asking for help is often looked down upon, Africans view it as an expression of what it means to share a common humanity.

Generally, you do not visit a village without the host sharing their food and gifts. This does not mean sharing from plenty. On the contrary, it means sharing what one has. It means sharing in a common humanity. Westerners who visit African churches may not know that people will prepare a feast for visitors (usually chicken or a goat), even if it is the last animal in that community. They would give live animals to a visitor even when that person is economically 2000 percent better off. Sharing in Bantu communities is not a sign of need or plenty. It is an expression of common humanity. Given this,

---

6. Cited in Michael Battle, *Reconciliation: The Ubuntu Theology of Desmond Tutu* (Cleveland: Pilgrim Press, 1997), 36.

7. According to Stanlake J.T. Samkange and Tommie M. Samkange, the Shona consider land as sacred (*zvinoyera*) and "the real owner of the land [to be] the tutelary spirit, *Mwari* and, to a lesser extent, the various tribal spirits." Stanlake J.T. Samkange and Tommie M. Samkange, *Hunhuism or Ubuntuism: A Zimbabwe Indigenous Political Philosophy* (Salisbury, Rhodesia: Graham Pub., 1980), 51–55.

it is considered an insult to refuse gifts even if given by a very poor person. Knowing this background helps us negotiate disciplined sharing. Let us hear the stories.

Hearing Each Other

Sierra Leone

They were traveling in northern Sierra Leone with a group from the mission agency USPG, visiting a village to see work of the Church and Community Mobilizing Process (CCMP).[8] After visiting the rice fields and hearing about increased production because of CCMP, the visitors were invited to join the villagers for a meal of rice, stew, and coconuts. When the meal was finished, the women began to dance. The guests watched, mesmerized by the rhythm and beauty of their dance to the beat of a single drum. Some longed to join them, but knew they could not match the simple yet beautiful movements. Suddenly they realized that one of the older ladies was beckoning them to join in. She had seen their fascination with the dance. Hesitantly, they approached the dancing women and the same lady began to show the movements. The outsiders became part of what they were creating—movements in praise of God in this mixed Muslim and Christian village. The visitors were never the best dancers but that did not matter. This was not about creating a perfect performance. It was about creating community as food and dance were shared.

At its heart, this story is about opening people's lives and communities across difference. It was a profound experience of sharing, and God was at the center. What drew the groups together was a shared identity and humanity despite differences in social and economic location. The invitation to join the dance was significant. Dance was at the heart of that community and the way they expressed welcome and friendship to outsiders. The invitation to a

---

8. A process to build and release local community resources to enable development toward self-sustainability.

Westerner to join them was sacrificial. It was much better when they were dancing on their own because they knew the movements instinctively. They were sacrificing excellence in performance in the interests of building community and incorporating the visitors into the wider human community. The visitors had the right to refuse in order to save their embarrassment. Sharing in the dance, however, the visitors gave themselves to the people and became one with them.

The invitation to join the dance echoes Trinitarian relationships. Rublev's icon of the Holy Trinity shows a circle with an opening. It is as though there is space for another to join the holy three. Just as the women in Sierra Leone invited outsiders into their dance, so we are invited to participate in the life of God the Holy Trinity. This invitation is about joining the mission of God as God's people in the world. It is about going and building relationships across the boundaries and barriers that humanity erects. It is about being agents or ambassadors in the communication of the love of the Holy Trinity in God's world.

Zambia and Bath and Wells Link

A link had existed between a parish in Bath and Wells diocese in England and a parish in Eastern Zambia for some time. In the English diocese there was a key person who facilitated communication and organized visits between the two parishes. It was a tragedy when this person died suddenly. The Zambian parish wanted to grieve for their friend but were unable to attend her funeral in England. So at the same time as the funeral was happening in England, the Zambian church gathered in their church to mourn the loss of their friend and to pray for their brothers and sisters in England. Listening to those involved in England and Zambia, the experience of mourning together was a deep entering into each other's loss and pain which made strong friendships even stronger.

This experience is about friendship across cultural boundaries. It is a disciplined sharing that will never be forgotten. This story is told many times beyond those directly involved and is a recent example of those words from Paul we have already met: if one suffers everyone suffers (1 Cor. 12:26). Such expressions of friendship happen because of God's love in the hearts of God's followers. Friendships were built through visits and sharing each other's lives.

What these stories have in common is that faith was grown and developed through cross-cultural encounters. Through disciplined sharing, communion is expressed. Friendship in Christ grows discipleship. As Christians share through worship, giving, visiting, Bible study, and reflection, so faith is deepened and Christians are equipped to participate in God's mission in the world.

Companion Link Relationships across the Anglican Communion

From 2014 to 2016, Janice conducted a research project into three companion link relationships across the Anglican Communion. Observation in the case studies showed the potential for two movements to happen when cross-cultural encounters occur and where there is genuine openness to other people and cultures. The first is that *the world shrinks*. When encountering someone from another culture, places that previously existed only on a map are personalized. A place becomes connected with a person or community. It is usually differences that are explored initially, but then similarities are discovered and explored between vastly different cultures. This process involves each finding and recognizing the other's humanity and recognizing something of us all in the "other" person. When this happens, an encounter that has the potential for transformation and growth in discipleship occurs.

The second movement is that *perceptions of God expand and grow*. As shared humanity and faith are discovered, so perceptions of God change. As people realize how large and small the world is, so perceptions of God expand. God is understood as over all and holding all things together (Eph. 1:10). This movement in discipleship has the greatest potential when there is a creative dynamic between cross-cultural encounters in scripture, prayer, and worship. All these elements are vital for the growth of both individuals and churches. A cross-cultural encounter can happen anywhere and does not have to involve traveling great distances. Meeting and interchange can move individuals and communities to more creative and life-giving thought and practice.

What about money? Financial donations are a very important way of giving but are not the only way. In the same research it was found that giving money best takes place within the context of friendship. In a world of great disparity, it is easy for the financially richer partner to dominate the relationship, even when this is not intended, and leave the partner with fewer financial resources wondering what they can give. The giving of financial resources needs to be disciplined, which means sometimes holding back from giving financially if the spirit of a companion link or friendship is to be honored. However, solely giving financially is legitimate and can be done through an aid agency if this is the preferred way of sharing.

Undisciplined sharing can lead to the dependence syndrome. Financial needs abound, but we should also realize that these resources are slowly disappearing in the global North. As the northern Sierra Leone story shows, disciplined sharing empowers churches in the global South to be self-funding. Sharing is a two-way process—we share what we have out of our love for one another. The gift to the Jerusalem church was for a limited period. It is our duty to empower one another through the act of sharing. Undisciplined sharing can easily become imperialistic. The cultural differences and social expectations between Christians in the global North and South have sometimes led to hostility among Christians.

Just as we hear of misappropriation of donated funds by African governments, such accusations occur among churches. Although in some cases this is true, it is important to educate each other on expectations and responsibilities, including the reporting procedures. We believe that sharing financial resources must be built around transparency and Christian love. Donated funds have led to hostility between bishops, priests, and parishioners. In the age of social media and the internet, miscommunication can lead to misinformation. Disciplined sharing demands trust and transparency. Since popular African perceptions of the church in Europe and North America are that it has a lot of money, the news of money shared makes people believe that millions of dollars and pounds are donated by link parishes. Just as transparency is now demanded in foreign aid, churches must do the same.

Questions for Reflection

5. Think of cross-cultural relationships that have grown and developed in your experience. What do you need from your link parish or diocese?
6. What helped these relationships grow and develop?
7. How can financial giving assist building friendships in Christ across social, cultural, and economic divides?
8. What is the place of scripture, prayer, and worship in building cross-cultural friendships?
9. What are some of the hindrances to sharing?

Hearing the Spirit

Through the Incarnation, God shared our humanity and invited us to be incarnational in how we deal with one another. At the center of the church's worship is the celebration of this costly divine sharing. The sharing of God to us is celebrated in the Holy Communion. We who are many are one body, for we share one bread (1 Cor. 10:17). The eucharistic ritual reminds us that we are one community celebrating God's self-giving to all (Phil. 2:6).

Sharing is an act of worship in which we are invited to take part. As we share the body of Christ with one another, we participate in God's mission in God's world. As we have already mentioned, there are many historical and contemporary forces that inhibit sharing. Our perceptions of each other's culture can so often be influenced by cultural ignorance, apathy, suspicion, misunderstanding, hostility, and colonial history. But living out communion calls Christians to see each other through the eyes of Jesus. This is not always easy. Christians can be critical and fail to see each other with the loving eyes of God. Christians must look beyond differences, beyond the values of the world to see each other with the eyes of Jesus Christ. Sharing in all its forms is a spiritual discipline. It is something that is done because to be aware of another person or community is to see the world beyond ourselves. This is how Christians grow in faith. Paul, again writing to the Corinthians, sums up this discipline: "Each of you must give as you have made up your mind, not reluctantly or under compulsion, for God loves a cheerful giver" (2 Cor. 9:7).

Below are some suggestions for bringing together action and contemplation in the discipline of sharing.

Meditating on the Fruits of the Spirit

The "fruit of the Spirit is love, joy, peace, patience, kindness, generosity, faithfulness, gentleness and self–control" (Gal. 5:22–23). All of these fruits of the Spirit are about generosity and they are necessary for building relationships and friendships. This is a practical list of the virtues necessary for building friendship in Christ.

Meditate on Galatians 5:22–23 and ask yourself where you are using these virtues to connect with people different from yourself and to build new relationships. Which of these virtues do you express readily? Which do you find more difficult? Bring to God any hesitations, fears, and failures and ask for forgiveness when you are convicted.

Pray for those you have already connected with in Christ's friendship and generosity. Prayerfully consider the outreach in which your church is engaged. How does this witness to friendship in Christ?

Meditation on the Rublev Icon[9]

Take time to be silent. Prayerfully reflect on the figures and the scene that depicts the hospitality of Abraham in Genesis 18. Meditate on the Rublev icon (or another icon or image of the Trinity that is available to you). Think of how God has shown generosity to you and welcomed you into God's life. How do you experience God's life and love as an individual and as a community?

Questions for Reflection

10. Where are you connecting with people of faith traditions different from your own?

---

9. You can find a picture of the icon here: https://en.wikipedia.org/wiki/Trinity_ (Andrei_Rublev), accessed August 14, 2019.

11. What acts of generosity have you shown to others recently?

12. Consider your practices of giving prayerfully. Have you reached a balance between your resources and your giving?

13. What acts of hospitality have you shown this week to those who are strangers and those known to you?

14. Look for examples of generosity and hospitality in your community. Could you receive a gift from a person or group poorer than yourself? Reflect on the nature of giving and receiving gifts. Do you find it easier to give gifts than to receive them from others?

Sharing the Earth

"All creation is a family of ecologically interconnected beings," Archbishop Thabo Makgoba wrote in his foreword to *Creation Care in Christian Mission*.[10] As a family of creatures, we cannot speak of disciplined sharing without addressing the refusal to share God's earth with other creatures. Such refusal has resulted in human-induced ecological crises that drive species into extinction, put the poor at risk, and threaten all future generations. The very concept of "common life" calls for sharing. Yet the global ecological crisis testifies to our refusal to share the earth and earth's natural goods.

In "The World Is Our Host," Anglican bishops noted that "attending to the current and future life and health of our planet will require sacrifices now, both personal and collective, a deeper appreciation of the interdependence of all creation, and a genuine commitment to repentance, reconciliation and redemption."[11] In this regard, the concept of disciplined sharing speaks to the Anglican fifth mark of mission. That mark calls us to "strive to safeguard the integrity of creation, and sustain and renew the life of the earth." Here is a call to care for creation just as we care for one another. As God's missioners,

10. Thabo Makgoba, foreword to *Creation Care in Christian Mission*, ed. Kapya J. Kaoma (Oxford: Regnum Studies in Mission, 2016), xiii.

11. The Anglican Consultative Council and the Anglican Communion Environmental Network, "The World Is Our Host: A Call to Urgent Action for Climate Justice," Good Friday 2015, 5: https://acen.anglicancommunion.org/media/148818/The-World-is-our-Host-FINAL-TEXT.pdf.

we are all invited to share the earth's resources with the poor and all creatures. In this regard, we need to pay attention to the needs of the wider earth community. As humans, we must realize that the creator owns the earth and its natural goods. We need to share the ecological burden that threatens the existence of all life on earth. In *Abundant Life*, Sallie McFague writes:

> By destroying the health of nature, we are undermining our own. The ecological [society] does not support either/or thinking: either my good or yours, either our good or nature's. The good life for nature— a resilient, complex nature—is what we must have for our good life, but our good life rests on our caring for nature's well-being.[12]

Together we are invited to care for the earth as our common home. In fact, disciplined sharing ought to enhance earth care while opposing policies that destroy the earth. Aside from campaigning against policies that harm the earth and the poor, global North Christians should share the ecological burden of poor nations. In *Creation Care in Christian Mission*, Kapya Kaoma writes:

> Tree-planting and land reclamation are some of the Earth-healing initiatives that ought to typify global Christian partnerships and witness. In the past, Christian unity has been witnessed in efforts to combat racism, HIV/AIDS, poverty and other social ills. Today, we need Christian unity in the fight against environmental degradation. Since most Africans depend on wood for fuel, for example, there is a need to encourage and partner with them to plant two trees for every tree felled. In addition, there is a need to help poor people access solar power. Just as Christian communities have partnered in safe-water provision to the poor, we need Christian partnership in the provision of solar power to the Earth's poor.[13]

---

12. Sallie McFague, *Life Abundant: Rethinking Theology and Economy for a Planet in Peril* (Minneapolis, MN: Fortress Press, 2007), 118.
13. Kapya J. Kaoma, *Creation Care in Christian Mission* (Oxford: Regnum Studies in Mission, 2016), 294.

Disciplined sharing extends to how we lead our everyday lives. As the gap between the rich and the poor continues to grow, all need to share simple lifestyles. For instance, during Lent, link partners in the global North can share the lifestyles of Christians in Africa by living on less than $2 a day. The money saved can then be donated to mission initiatives for earth care. Such initiatives might include establishing a "link garden" or forest to be named after the link parish or diocese. For example, the Zambian Church link with the Diocese of Bath and Wells can pay for tree planting projects in Zambia from the money saved from sharing simple lifestyles. This type of sharing will increase our solidarity with the poor while healing the earth. Lest we forget, the Christ who invites us to share our common life on earth is also the source of all life. Through him all things were made (John 1:3; Col. 1:16).

Questions for Reflection

15. In what ways can disciplined sharing enhance mission partnerships across the globe?
16. Where is earth care in your missional goals as an individual, as a parish, and as a diocese?
17. How can the church work to enhance earth care?
18. To what extent do you agree with Archbishop Makgoba's claim that "all creation is a family of ecologically interconnected beings"? What are the implications for disciplined sharing in your context?

Structures get bad press. We have been arguing, however, that disciplined sharing, and the structures they depend upon, are important for effective Christian witness. Many people think of structures as unnecessary and inhibiting to the life of the Spirit. As we have seen, the early church established structures, councils, networks, procedures, and leaders. The problem arises when the structures become too important in and of themselves and hinder the service of others. In such cases there is need to rethink how these structures can be reformed to enhance the accountability of the giver and the receiver.

The structures of the Anglican Communion are summed up in the Lambeth Quadrilateral: episcopacy, scripture, the historic creeds, and the sacraments of

Eucharist and baptism. The purpose of the Anglican Consultative Council (ACC) is to enable disciplined sharing across the Anglican Communion through representation from all provinces. The ACC is an important expression of the body of Christ as it includes laypeople as well as clergy and bishops. The Lambeth Conference of bishops, which is in preparation now for the 2020 conference, expresses the collegiality of the bishops of the Communion and their leadership in mission. The Anglican Communion Office enables a vast amount of disciplined sharing through its committees and advisory structures. All of these bodies or structures enable order, which is a shared understanding of faith, belief, identity, and practice so that the church can connect with and be part of God's mission in the world.

The companion link relationships between dioceses across the Communion significantly encourage and enable disciplined sharing that builds churches and expresses what it means to be the body of Christ. These far-reaching links cannot be practiced in Anglican isolation. Ecumenically, the World Council of Churches is important as a structure that enables disciplined sharing between the world communions. As Christians, we not only share the gospel with others—we share our traditions and lives also. In this regard, disciplined sharing is central to what it means for Anglicans to witness to God's generosity.

6

Communion as a Discipleship
of Mutuality

Cornelia Eaton and James Stambaugh

T his chapter is about mutuality and the practices of discipleship that
lead to mutuality. Cornelia Eaton, one author of this chapter, is *Diné*.
The *Diné* are indigenous people whose ancient home is in the southwestern
region of what is now called the United States of America.[1] Cornelia lives
just outside of Farmington, New Mexico, in and with land that has been
home to her family for a long time. Cornelia grew up as an Episcopalian
but was also taught by her mother and grandmother to respect and practice the traditional ways of the *Diné*. James Stambaugh, the other author of
this chapter, is Anglo and was born in northern New Mexico about three
hours away from Farmington. We met briefly at an Episcopal church in
New Mexico but got to know each other when we both became students at
Virginia Theological Seminary in Alexandria, Virginia. It was there, far away
from our homes, that we first began talking about the themes of this chapter.

Our understanding of mutuality has always been connected to food. We
talk a lot about the unique cuisine of New Mexico, which owes much to both
Hispanic/Latino and indigenous cultures. More than talking about food,

---

1. In our own language, *Diné* means "the people." Spanish colonists who moved into
the homeland of the *Diné* in the 1600s called us the Navajo. This is the Spanish deri-
vation of the word *Tewa*, which is from another indigenous language and means "large
area of cultivated land." See J. Lee Correll, *Through White Men's Eyes: A Contribution
to Navajo History* (Window Rock, AZ: Navajo Times, 1976).

however, our understanding of mutuality has been shaped by the act of sharing meals—lunch in the seminary refectory, supper with family and friends, and the eucharistic meal around the altar.

One of the traditional practices of the *Diné* is to make yarn from sheep's wool and to weave intricate tapestries and rugs. We intend to do something similar here, weaving together indigenous wisdom, our own different life experiences, and the many threads that make up the church's encounter with the Risen Savior in the breaking open of scripture and the breaking of bread. We are inspired by the image of the weaver taking different threads of many colors and qualities and from the many crafting one—a beautiful and harmonious whole. This is a good way to imagine the Christian discipleship of mutuality. The prophet Isaiah uses the image of God as a potter, shaping and forming us like clay (Isa. 64:8). We have in mind a related image of God the master artisan. God is the weaver. We are the threads. We begin with the strongest thread we have: the mighty cord of scripture.

Hearing Scripture

> *If then there is any encouragement in Christ, any consolation from love, any sharing in the Spirit, any compassion and sympathy, make my joy complete: be of the same mind, having the same love, being in full accord and of one mind. Do nothing from selfish ambition or conceit, but in humility regard others as better than yourselves. Let each of you look not to your own interests, but to the interests of others. Let the same mind be in you that was in Christ Jesus,*
> *who, though he was in the form of God,*
> *did not regard equality with God*
> *as something to be exploited,*
> *but emptied himself,*
> *taking the form of a slave,*
> *being born in human likeness.*
> *And being found in human form,*
> *he humbled himself*

and became obedient to the point of death—
even death on a cross.
Therefore God also highly exalted him
and gave him the name
that is above every name,
so that at the name of Jesus
every knee should bend,
in heaven and on earth and under the earth,
and every tongue should confess
that Jesus Christ is Lord,
to the glory of God the Father.

(Phil. 2:1–11)

This passage from Philippians chapter two provides a working biblical definition of mutuality and offers insight into the practice of a discipleship of
mutuality for Christians, including Anglican Christians in the twenty-first
century. Mutuality is having the same mind as Christ, having the same love,
and being in full accord with each other.

Having the same mind as Christ is not simply mental or intellectual agreement with Christ. Rather, it is union. Union with Christ does not begin with us
at all, but with the love that Christ has for us. According to Philippians, Christ's
love is where we find the encouragement and consolation that we access and
participate in through the working of the Holy Spirit in our individual and corporate lives. Only through God's grace in Jesus Christ given to us by the Spirit
can we truly have the same mind, and the same love for each other, being in full
accord with each other. Only through grace can we participate in mutuality.

Having the same mind as Christ Jesus does not mean that we will be able
to read each other's thoughts, or that we will always agree with each other as
Christian sisters and brothers. In Philippians 2, the Greek word that is translated as "same mind/one mind" means "having thoughts with the same intent."
This does not mean that every thought must be identical, or that we must
always agree with each other. Having the same mind as Christ Jesus means

having the same thoughtful intention toward each other: mutual concern for each other with the intent to care for each other with our words and actions. It is about sharing the same intention to act in love—that same love that Christ has for all of us. Having the same mind means that we all must agree only to offer ourselves to each other, to care for each other, and to regard each other more than we regard ourselves, just as Christ emptied himself and offered himself on our behalf.

Having the same mind and same love is rooted in right action toward each other. This means acting unselfishly toward each other, actively regarding the other as better than ourselves, and looking toward the interest of others instead of our own. This is what biblical mutuality means.

Our actions toward each other are informed by intent, and our intent is shaped by our wills and desires. For mutuality to occur, then, our wills and desires must be formed through good habits, through encounter with scripture, and through the stories, prayers, and liturgies that inspire our imaginations toward wholeness and peace. All of this is part of the practice of discipleship toward mutuality. Philippians 2 informs our discipleship toward mutuality by first offering us an example to follow. Verses 6–11 comprise a hymn that praises Christ for the self-emptying he underwent in order to become human for us. Christ is our example. True Christian discipleship and mutuality begin and end in him.

Mutuality occurs when we find each other, not in the merging or blending of our individual personalities, but when we are together in union with our Lord. We meet each other in true mutuality when we each have met Jesus and seek to follow him together in the way of discipleship, which is the way of the cross (Mark 8:34). Jesus entered human history by emptying himself, taking on the form of a servant and the likeness of humanity in order to dwell among us (John 1:14). Christ's journey toward us is the way of mutuality. This way that Jesus took led to the cross and to resurrection. In order to follow Jesus and take up our own cross, we must empty ourselves of selfish ambition and of the impulse to only look after our own needs, and instead regard the needs of others first. When we empty ourselves, we open ourselves up to see that we are interdependent on each other and dependent on God. This all happens on the way of Jesus, the way of the cross. We discern our mutuality, our interdependence upon one another, when we are able to see that the way of the cross is "none other than the way of life and peace."[2]

Questions for Reflection

1. How do we make joy complete according to Philippians? What are the biblical practices that lead to perfect joy?
2. What are some of the good habits we can create that will shape our wills, desires, and imaginations toward having the same mind as Christ Jesus?
3. Having the mind of Christ does not mean that we must agree on all things, but rather that we must share the same thoughtful intention of love toward each other. What implications does this have for us when we encounter disagreements in our personal lives, churches, and Communion?
4. What does "emptying oneself" or "taking up one's cross" look like in different contexts? Does this mean the same thing for those living in poverty or for who have been oppressed as it does for someone living in comfort and luxury?

Hearing Each Other

Hozhó and Discipleship

The *Diné* have a cherished life principle that parallels and interweaves—like a spider's web, or like the weaving of wool yarn into a rug—with the way of discipleship that leads to true mutuality. This principle/way of life is called *hozhó*. It is difficult to translate this word into English. A simplified translation is "the beauty way" or "the harmony way." *Hozhó* is the way that leads toward harmony with all people, with all of creation, and with the creator. It

---

2. The Episcopal Church, "A Collect for Fridays," in *The Book of Common Prayer and the Administration of the Sacraments and Other Rites and Ceremonies of the Church* (New York: Church Publishing Incorporated, 1979), 99, https://www.episcopal church.org/files/book_of_common_prayer.pdf.

is a way of life. It is a way of seeing the world that includes rituals and prayers. It shapes a person toward unity, peace, and fellowship.

Hozhó describes the deep reality of interconnectedness that binds all people with creation and with God. "The beauty way" is the daily journey that a person must follow toward wholeness in concert with the universe. It describes the way toward mutual relationships, where people find peace when they open their hearts and minds to others in love and compassion. The definition of *hozhó* is both very personal and very broad. The harmony of "the beauty way" extends beyond interpersonal relationships to our relationship with all of creation and to the entire cosmos. "The beauty way" is meant to lead toward the harmony of all creation, and yet, we see much chaos in this world. The dream of harmony can easily be lost. If we are paying attention, we can glimpse fleeting moments of the beauty way in the midst of the chaos. This means that some of the habits that we must acquire are those that will help us to pay attention to what is happening around us. We need to develop the eyes that will see what God is doing in the world so that we can see the beauty way that unfolds around us in unexpected ways. The challenge is to pay attention.

It is often in a state of brokenness that these fleeting moments of *hozhó* are revealed. Given the nature of Jesus's incarnation, this should not be surprising. According to Paul, Jesus emptied himself and joined us in the human condition. Mutuality begins with sharing in the brokenness of humanity. Brokenness can mean many things. It can mean loneliness, a feeling of isolation, not being welcome in society or in a group, or it can mean the feeling of absence or loss. Within this chaos that we all experience, we must learn to be in "the beauty way" by understanding how our wholeness, mutuality, and peace come from Jesus, despite the chaos and isolation we find within ourselves. Peace happens out of our experiences of brokenness, hurt, and chaos. "The beauty way" is about the transformation that occurs by God's grace, even in the midst of these experiences.

In Genesis, as the Spirit hovers over the waters of chaos; God speaks all of creation into existence. Christians believe that Jesus is the Word that speaks everything into being and sustains all things. One specific practice of *hozhó* mirrors this theology of creation and offers insight into how we are invited to join God by walking in the way. There is a particular "beauty way" ceremony for *Diné* women. It is when we are sung into a new way of becoming. Like the creation story, chaos in our own lives is sung into order through the course of the ceremony, which takes place in a *hogan*.[3] The ceremony is for an individual who needs to be reconciled or restored to harmony. For this to happen, this person's community must gather as a family. There is no restoration without community. The yucca root, one of the sacred plants, is used to wash the hair and body of the person who is undergoing the ceremony. After the washing of purification, "the beauty way" song is chanted. Every part of the person, from the bottom of their feet to the top of their head, and everything they put on— moccasins, clothing, silver and turquoise jewelry, and the hair tie for a traditional hair bun—is incorporated into the song of transformation. It is about the transformation of our relationships with ourselves, with creation, and with God. When the song is over, the person is transformed. Yet the transformation must continue with the person and with the entire community after everyone has left the *hogan*. It is up to everyone to go out and live in the way of *hozhó*, to be in relationship with all of God's people.

As *Diné* Christians, we recognize that there are a lot of parallels between "the beauty way" ceremony and baptism. The one does not replace the other, but the one may illuminate the other. Christians, in baptism, are called to discipleship and called to an empowering and commissioning into God's world as God's people, to live in God's harmony and in mutuality in God's creation. For *Diné*, as for many cultures, stories and songs are part of what empowers us and emboldens us for this work of such discipleship. Stories and songs weave us together and help us to see our common humanity. Part of discipleship is learning to see God in the story so that we can also discern our common dependence on God and God's grace.

---

3. A *hogan* is a traditional *Diné* dwelling place, and a place where ceremonies are performed. *Hogans* are constructed to align with the four sacred directions and made to facilitate a sacred circle of listening.

When Cornelia first arrived at seminary, she had a difficult time adjusting. She missed her family, and the four sacred mountains that surround the home of the *Diné*, in each of the four directions. She slowly became accustomed to this new land, a new community, and new people. One Friday, a month into the fall academic term, Cornelia was in the hallway outside the common kitchen of her seminary dorm. There she encountered a group of seminary students from several nations in East Africa. Cornelia sensed that like her, these students were in a period of adjustment, having come far from their homes to study, in what sometimes felt like a strange land. Like her, she thought, they might also long for their homeland. These students—several from Tanzania and one from Kenya—were gathered in the kitchen of the dorm preparing a meal to share with each other. The meal consisted of ingredients and leftovers from the seminary's refectory prepared with East African methods and spices. When these students noticed Cornelia in the doorway, they immediately invited her to join them. Cornelia watched as they finished preparing the meal. They made dough in a saucepan, which they then put in the middle of the table with meat and vegetables from the refectory that they had fixed up. They invited Cornelia to sit around the common table with them and eat. As they all sat down, one student offered to find Cornelia a fork. Cornelia realized that her hosts were planning to eat with their hands, but they didn't want her to be uncomfortable. Cornelia responded, "I don't need a fork. I used to eat like this with my paternal grandmother and family. I still eat like this. It's how I remember the old ways."

They all ate together. Cornelia, as the guest, was invited to take the first piece of the bread made from rice dough. Eating this way, though she was following the lead of her friends from a very different culture than her own, she felt somehow like they were helping her connect to the traditional ways of her own people. Though each culture is unique, there was in that moment a shared connection between *Diné* and East African cultures. The basis for that connection was a gentle hospitality and a simple but generous openness. Cornelia felt at home for the first time at seminary. She knew that these fellow students were family. She describes this as an experience of *hozhó*. It was an experience of harmony that went beyond circumstance to forge a connection with others that was bigger than all the things that separated them. Eating at the same table and dipping into the same bowl—they found they were God's family. In this moment, Cornelia felt she was in "the beauty way," where there was potential for healing and wholeness. Loneliness and isolation did not have the final word. It was a moment of peace in a foreign land. This experience of *hozhó* began with an invitation and an openness to share with another. This seemingly quotidian gesture opened the door for God's grace to meet those gathered around the table.

Questions for Reflection

5. What simple gesture of hospitality and openness do you or can you perform in your context?
6. How can these gestures lead to deeper experiences of mutuality with others across differences?

Internal and personal chaos is not the only type of chaos through which *hozhó* might emerge. There is a chaos that results from societal and structural sin. There is systemic evil that ensnares, confuses, and alienates us on a societal scale. The treatment of *Diné* and other Native Americans by the United States government has been shameful. The Episcopal Church has been complicit in this mistreatment. One example of this is the practice of forcibly removing children from their homes and sending them to boarding schools where they were not allowed to practice their traditional ways and languages. From the 1870s right up until the late twentieth century, the US government contracted with several Christian denominations to run these boarding schools. There, native children were forced to assimilate to Anglo culture. In addition to the intrinsic violence of these schools—attempting to destroy native culture and identity—there have been many documented cases of physical abuse.[4] The Episcopal Church was responsible for at least fourteen of these boarding schools, including schools with *Diné* students.[5] The full story of this tragic and sinful practice is yet to be told. The Episcopal Church has much reckoning yet to do with this chapter of her history. These and many more examples of marginalization, oppression, and worse raise a difficult question. Is Christian mutuality possible in light of such injustice? Can *hozhó*, "the beauty way," be seen even in cases of systemic evil?

Questions for Reflection

7. What are the practices that create and sustain mutuality in a broken world where we are mired in systems of injustice? How can we have the mind of Christ in a world so shattered by sin?

8. How does the example of Christ in Philippians 2 speak to Anglos, and to others who find themselves to be the beneficiaries of systemic sin?

In the midst of such mire, we glimpse "the beauty way" in the remarkable resilience of indigenous peoples, cultures, languages, and wisdom. The *Diné* have survived and thrived in very difficult circumstances and despite frequent marginalization and mistreatment. The Episcopal Church in Navajoland, though small and lacking the resources of many other dioceses in the United States, possesses a wellspring of patience and creativity. More and more its strength lies in the *Diné* leaders, clergy and laity, who are empowered and trained to do the work of the church and be agents of God's reconciliation in their communities. Because of this resilience and leadership, graced partnerships have emerged between Navajoland, other parts of the Episcopal Church, and the wider community. One example of resilient creative leadership is a start-up enterprise called Cheii's Web Development. Cheii's trains young *Diné* in web development, computer programming, and social media marketing skills, and brings economic opportunities to places where there

---

4. David Foster Adams, *Education for Extinction: American Indians and the Boarding School Experience, 1875–1928* (Lawrence: University Press of Kansas, 1995).

5. G. Jeffrey MacDonald, "A Shocking History," *The Living Church*, February 28, 2018, https://livingchurch.org/2018/02/28/a-shocking-history/.

are few. This enterprise began in partnership with the Episcopal Church in Navajoland. Through this partnership, other Episcopal churches and dioceses have partnered with Cheii's, notably the Episcopal Diocese of Pennsylvania. Farmington, New Mexico, and Pennsylvania are about 1,700 miles away, and yet the Diocese of Pennsylvania is able to contract with Cheii's to provide web development services to its mission churches and other congregations who benefit from this valuable resource. It is neither a cut-and-dried business partnership nor a wealthy (mostly Anglo) diocese "helping" the less wealthy indigenous diocese. Here, the beginnings of mutuality are found in honest partnership that values each party equally.

The *Diné* way of reading scripture and teaching has its basis in storytelling. *Diné* culture is still something of an oral culture. *Diné* build a story like they build a "beauty way" basket out of yucca plant. The story begins at the center. It begins with the key point, person, event, or detail, and then the story spirals out from there in ever widening circles. The story turns around on itself many times, winding and weaving, but it also extends, slowly but surely, outward. As Christians, the center of our story is Christ. It is the Christ at the center of the hymn in Philippians 2, the Christ who teaches us how to live in harmony and mutuality with each other. Christ emptied himself of all the glory of heaven and became human in order to make us whole. Christ gives us the grace and power to follow him in this way. The story of Christ's transforming power then spirals out, first into our own personal lives, then into our families and close friends, then our communities, our churches and dioceses, and in ever broadening circles from there. We can hardly guess or dare imagine how far it extends.

The discipleship of mutuality enables us to be woven into this story. Ever mindful that the center is Christ, we can find ourselves caught up in this great story of God's redemption and discover how we can be participants in God's weaving work. Caught up in God's web and weft, we look around and discover our interconnectedness with each other, despite our differences. This is reflected in the *Diné* principle of *hozhó*, "the way of beauty" through which one discovers harmony and peace with all creation and with the creator. What remains is to briefly explore some of the practices and tangible ways that we can allow ourselves to be woven into God's tapestry of mutuality.

Hearing the Spirit

Practices toward Mutuality

Discipleship that leads to mutuality refers to the bodily and spiritual practices that lead to various and different people sharing the mind of Christ and sharing the same love. Philippians 2 shows us that the self-giving Christ is the center and the source of this way of discipleship. Like "the beauty way" basket, we begin with the center and discover how practices of discipleship transform us personally, and then show how to live in harmony with those around us in ever widening spirals.

Entering into the way of beauty and the way of discipleship that comes from Jesus must begin with prayer. Prayer activates mutuality. For those who have been marginalized, a deep practice of prayer is essential to finding a place of resilience, strength, and forgiveness. For those who benefit from the marginalization of others, Christ is calling them to the self-emptying way of the cross. In response to this call, the practice of contemplative prayer is an important and generative starting place. Prayer of this sort asks us to sit before God and open ourselves up to God's transforming power. Over time this prayer life invites God into every single part of our lives. For anyone who finds themselves in the midst of chaos and turmoil, contemplative prayer can anchor them in the peace that passes all understanding, the peace that only comes from Jesus Christ.

A place to begin on this way of discipleship is through simple meditative prayer practices. One might, in times of trouble or chaos, cry out, "Jesus help me," or following the practice of Eastern Christians, "Lord Jesus Christ, have mercy on me, a sinner."

A second, related practice of discipleship is the training of our hearts, minds, and bodies to sense the presence of the divine in creation. In *Diné* tradition, prayers are blessings offered in the *hogan* in which all share. The ceremonial dwelling symbolizes the whole universe in which all abide. So the prayers offered in the *hogan* are a blessing meant for all of creation, as those who offer prayers learn to recognize the spirit of the most holy one living and active in creation. Traditionally, prayer is offered at dawn, noon, evening, and night. This is known as "the four directions prayer." At each of these times, "the beauty way" prayer is extended in the four directions, reminding us to follow this path wherever we go. We say, *Tzo dizin binah nizhoni go naasha*, which means "It is because of prayer I walk in beauty." This is the invitation to walk and follow Jesus in the paths of the four directions of the harmony way. We are invited to walk with God, with ourselves, with humanity, and with all creation. Each step is a prayer, and the Holy Spirit prays with us and in us along the beauty way (Rom. 8:15–16, 26–27).

A third practice of discipleship is to have meals with people across differences. As we have seen, mutuality is mysteriously connected to food. Sharing a meal with another is a great way to discover a common bond. A shared meal is a great way to focus our attention on the present moment so that we can listen carefully. Intentionally sharing meals with those who are different from yourself can be a serious act of faithful discipleship. The acts of extending hospitality and accepting it both train us to be more open, more self-giving, more willing to acknowledge and understand our mutual interdependence on others and on God. The value and spiritual meaning of these acts are compressed and distilled in the sacramental meal of the Eucharist.

A fourth practice of discipleship toward mutuality is honing the art of listening to one another. This is where the practices that form our own thoughts, wills, and desires toward harmony and fellowship meet the reality of communal life. Listening is where we learn to encounter God in each other. The *Diné* phrase for this is "sitting in the sacred circle." When you sit down with others to listen deeply and attentively, you are creating a sacred circle. Jesus is present (Matt. 18:20) and Jesus teaches us how to do this. Jesus related to God the Father through his ears. Through withdrawal, and a sustaining practice of prayer, Jesus listened attentively to the Father. We must abide in Jesus's love, as he abides in the Father's, through listening to one another, and to God, with the same careful attention. When we do so, we discover that God speaks through each of us, and that we encounter God's grace in the sacred space created by listening.

A fifth practice of discipleship toward mutuality is shaping our imaginations through our stories. We must learn to understand our own personal narratives, our family histories, and the deep connections to places and people, in order to be interwoven with the great story of God's redemption for all of creation. One way this occurs is through the intentional and prayerful engagement of scripture in community. Hearing scripture together is a foundation for mutuality.

A sixth practice of discipleship for mutuality involves the hard work of partnering together for mission. Partnerships must be mutual—based on mutual strengths as well a mutual intent for the other's well-being. Partnerships for mission are, first and foremost, partnerships of listening. Partners must listen to God and try to discern what God is doing in the world. Then partners can discern their role in the work of God and how their own stories interweave with each other's to join into God's great tapestry of redemption.

Beauty Way Prayer (Traditional Diné Prayer)

Jesus Christ, young man chief, God's son,
Now your offering I have made; sacred mountain tobacco smoke
    I have made.
In beauty may I walk, all day long may I walk,
Through returning seasons may I walk,
On the trail marked with corn pollen may I walk,
With dew about my feet may I walk,
With beauty may I walk,
With beauty before me, may I walk,
With beauty behind me, may I walk,
With beauty above me, may I walk,
With beauty below me, may I walk,
With beauty all around me, may I walk.
In old age wandering on a trail of beauty, lively, may I walk.
In old age wandering on a trail of beauty, living again, may I
    walk.
In beauty it is finished, in beauty it is finished, in beauty it is
    finished, in beauty it is finished.

7

Communion and Ecumenical Questions

Anne Burghardt and John Gibaut

There is one body and one Spirit, just as you were called to the one hope of your calling, one Lord, one faith, one baptism, one God and Father of all, who is above all and through all and in all. But each of us was given grace according to the measure of Christ's gift.

(Eph. 4:4–7)

Hearing Scripture

From its earliest roots, the ecumenical impulse toward partnership, unity, and communion has been a biblical response to the deeply dysfunctional mission of the divided churches. How do divided churches, with their competing missionary and ecclesiological claims, bear faithful witness to the reconciling love of God in Jesus Christ, while they are not reconciled to one another (see 2 Cor. 5:18–20)? How do divided Christians bear witness to the biblical commitments to justice and peace, when they are the bearers of hatred and violence toward one another?

From the beginning, the search for Christian unity has been intrinsically linked to mission, as the prayer of Jesus on the night before his suffering and death so vividly proclaims: "The glory that you have given me I have given them, so that they may be one, as we are one, I in them and you in me, that they may become completely one, so that the world may know that you have sent me and have loved them even as you have loved me" (John 17:22–23). The history of Christian disunity, from the earliest days of the church to the present time, has been a contradiction of this biblical vision of unity and communion for the church, for humanity, and for the whole creation. The ecumenical journey that seeks the healing of ancient and modern divisions is grounded in the biblical hope of "one Lord, one faith, one baptism, one God and Father of all" (Eph. 4:4–7). The ecumenical movement has sought to embody the prayer of Jesus that his disciples may be one, so that the world may believe (John 17:21).

The biblical word that has most shaped the ecumenical vision of Christian unity is the Greek New Testament word *koinonia*. It is customarily translated with the English word "fellowship" but is best translated as "communion." A vital understanding of the church comes from the biblical concept of communion or *koinonia*. The Greek noun *koinonia* derives from the verb meaning "to have something in common," "to share," "to participate," "to have part in," or "to act together." It appears in passages recounting the sharing in the Eucharist (1 Cor. 10:16–17), the meaning of reconciliation (Gal. 2:7–10), the support of the poor (Rom. 15:26; 2 Cor. 8:3–4), and the experience and witness of the church (Acts 2:42–45). Paul understands this *koinonia* to be at the heart of the Triune God: "The grace of our Lord Jesus Christ, the love of God, and the communion of the Holy Spirit be with you all" (2 Cor. 13:13). Life in communion is intrinsically one of justice and peace. The church is called to make visible the irrevocable gift of God's communion within the human family, and indeed, with the whole created order.[1] The understanding of the Christian community, the church, as communion is one of the biblical insights that undergirds the question of Christian unity.

Questions for Reflection

1. Where does Christian disunity hurt in your context?
2. What prejudices or inherited memories do you have of other churches?
3. To what extent has your faith grown through contact with Christians from other churches?
4. What are the occasions when you pray for Christian unity?

---

1. Acts 2:24; Acts 4:32; Rom. 12:13; Rom. 15:26–27; 1 Cor. 1:9; 1 Cor. 10:16, 18–20; 2 Cor. 1:7; Phil. 1:3; Gal. 2:9; 1 Pet. 4:13; 1 John 1:3, 7.

Hearing Each Other

The Anglican-Lutheran Journey

Anglicans and Lutherans have heard the call of the ecumenical movement from its earliest days. From 1920 to the present, Anglicans, Lutherans, and their ecumenical partners have explored together issues around the unity and mission of the church as members of the Faith and Order movement, and with it, the World Council of Churches. With the arrival of the Roman Catholic Church into the ecumenical movement in the wake of the Second Vatican Council (1962–1965), a new kind of forum for ecumenical theological dialogue was created. A series of bilateral dialogues sought to resolve particular church-dividing issues with the intention of restoring full communion in Christian faith, life, worship, and mission. The Anglican Communion engaged also in bilateral dialogues with the Roman Catholic Church, the Orthodox and Oriental Orthodox Churches, the World Methodist Conference, the World Baptist Alliance, the World Alliance (now Communion) of Reformed Churches, and the Lutheran World Federation. In turn, the Lutheran World Federation (LWF) entered into a series of bilateral dialogues with the Roman Catholic Church, the Orthodox Church, the Mennonite World Conference, the World Communion of Reformed Churches, the Anglican Communion, and most recently the Pentecostal World Fellowship.

All of the vast networks of multilateral and bilateral relationships, with their theological dialogues, share the same ultimate goal—the restoration of full, visible communion in one faith and in one eucharistic fellowship. The interim results have increased trust, mutual love, and engagement in mission at the global, regional, and local levels. Anglican-Lutheran dialogue has led to a series of full communion relationships, starting in northern Europe and North America.

The Christian disunity associated with the sixteenth-century Reformation left memories of violent ruptures, religious wars, and condemnations of confessional theological positions. The modern ecumenical movement has had the tasks of resolving historical church-dividing issues and of healing memories. The achievements of the Anglican bilateral dialogues with Roman

Catholic, Orthodox, Oriental Orthodox, Methodist, Baptist, and Reformed Churches, and the Lutheran bilateral dialogues with Roman Catholic, Orthodox, Reformed, Mennonite, and Pentecostal Churches have been much celebrated, as they have enabled much healing.

Such histories and conversations, however, have not been features of Anglican-Lutheran dialogue. There simply were no Anglican-Lutheran mutual condemnations of one another, or any formal actions that signaled a breach in communion. In Europe, Anglicans and Lutherans were separated from each other geographically. There were only a few direct contacts between these churches over the centuries following the Reformation. The ecumenical movement has in a way brought these "cousins" who had almost forgotten about each other's existence closer—with the significant exception of prejudices about each other based on national identity. This very different ecumenical context explains why there have not been any dramatic reconciliation actions to note, such as the signing of the Joint Declaration on the Doctrine of Justification between the LWF and the Catholic Church in 1999; or the 2010 Lutheran-Mennonite Action in Stuttgart where Lutherans asked Mennonites for forgiveness for past condemnations and persecutions carried out during the Reformation; or the Lund Commemoration of the Reformation in 2016 in the presence of Pope Francis.

Unity in Mission

The long series of international dialogues between the Anglican Communion Office (ACO) and the Lutheran World Federation has been particularly fruitful. In many parts of the world, relationships of full communion have been established and lived out between Anglicans and Lutherans. In Northern Europe and the British Isles, as well as in North America, there are full communion agreements between the two traditions, which have increasingly come to appreciate each other's gifts that serve God's mission in the world. It is interesting to note that although the missiological concept of the *missio Dei*—God's mission—has not been the main topic of any of the LWF's ecumenical dialogues, the Anglican-Lutheran *Niagara Report* (1987) succeeded in tackling difficult questions of church order and ministry in the light of a theology of the gifts that God has given to his church for mission. This approach also bore fruit in the "Porvoo Common Statement," published under the title *Together in Mission and Ministry* (1993). In creating both of these texts, beginning with the *missio Dei* enabled a breakthrough on issues of ministry that had historically been some of the most disputed questions between the two traditions.[2]

The bilateral relationship that has achieved the most in restoring communion with the churches of the Anglican Communion has been with the churches of the LWF. On the eve of the Lambeth Conference of 2020, there are three regional relationships between Anglicans and Lutherans. The Porvoo Common Statement, *Together in Mission and Ministry*, exists between sixteen Anglican and Lutheran Churches in Britain and Ireland, and the Nordic and Baltic regions. The *Called to Common Mission* agreement exists between the Episcopal Church and the Evangelical Lutheran Church in America. The Waterloo Declaration exists between the Anglican Church of Canada and the Evangelical Lutheran Church in Canada. As both the titles and the contents of these agreements suggest, mission and communion are inextricably linked. In the summer of 2019, the two North American Anglican Churches and the two North American Lutheran Churches entered into full communion with each other.

These historic Anglican-Lutheran agreements are rooted in the earlier agreements within the Commission on Faith and Order of the World Council of Churches, especially in its landmark convergence text of 1982, *Baptism, Eucharist and Ministry*. They are also shaped by the results of the dialogues that Lutherans and Anglicans have shared separately with Roman Catholic, Orthodox, Methodist, and Reformed traditions. As such, Anglican and Lutheran reflection on mission and communion is a remarkable synthesis of ecumenical dialogue in these areas, which has much enriched both the churches of the Anglican Communion and the churches of the LWF.

---

2. Paul D.L. Avis, *A Ministry Shaped by Mission* (New York: T&T Clark International, 2005), 13.

The multilateral and bilateral dialogues have consistently moved the churches beyond the language of "partnership" toward the language of "communion" (*koinonia*). This understanding of communion starts within the love of the Triune God, is shared in creation, and is marred by human sin. In the paschal mystery of Christ, communion between humanity and God is irreversibly restored. It is shared between believers and effected in a particular way by baptism and by eucharistic fellowship (1 Cor. 10:16–17). It is a communion that reflects the mission of God in reconciliation (Gal. 2:7–10), in caring for the poor (Rom. 15:26; 2 Cor. 8:3–4), and in the witness of the church (Acts 2:42–45). Mission, then, belongs to the very being of the church as the body of Christ. The church's participation in God's mission is a gift of God's grace, a gift grounded in and flowing from the in-breaking reign of God in Christ. Created out of grace to be part of the divine communion, the church does not live for itself, but for God, for all people, and for creation. This mission includes sharing in a common journey with people in their contexts and focusing on transformation, reconciliation, and empowerment. These are expressions of God's Trinitarian mission as creator, redeemer, and sanctifier. However, understanding mission and the whole life of the church as participation in God's holistic mission has, at least for Lutherans, been a journey that included significant paradigm shifts.

Whereas at the Fourth Assembly of the LWF (Helsinki, 1963) mission was still defined as aiming at conversion from unbelief to faith, from the Sixth Assembly (Dar es Salaam, 1977) onward, mission was understood and practiced in a holistic way as encompassing proclamation, advocacy, and service to the whole person and to all people.[3] The Anglican Communion's ongoing reflection on mission is summarized in the five marks of mission, articulated by successive meetings of the Anglican Consultative Council.[4] Mission is:

---

3. At the Lutheran World Federation's Global Consultation on Mission (Nairobi, 1998), transformation was considered an important dimension of mission.
4. "Marks of Mission," Anglican Communion, accessed March 29, 2019, http://www.anglicancommunion.org/mission/marks-of-mission.aspx.

1. To proclaim the Good News of the Kingdom
2. To teach, baptize, and nurture new believers
3. To respond to human need by loving service
4. To transform unjust structures of society, to challenge violence of every kind and pursue peace and reconciliation
5. To strive to safeguard the integrity of creation, and sustain and renew the life of the earth

Participation in God's mission is a gift of God's grace. Therefore, the churches are called to ecumenically join their efforts in serving God and the world. The LWF document *Mission in Context: Transformation. Reconciliation. Empowerment* (2004) offers a representative view of the LWF's understanding of mission. It declares that the "tendency to compete for mission fields in different parts of the world, in the race to expand the profile and sphere of influence of one's own denomination or organization, should be replaced by cooperation and joint action. Competition and the idea of 'conquest,' as well as proselytism, jeopardize and undermine God's mission."[5] The spirit of competition and spheres of influence should be replaced not only by cooperation and joint action but also by joint reflection and prayer, and by sharing of gifts, as God's gifts grow and bear more fruit when shared with others. Joint participation in God's mission also requires joint reflection on holistic mission. This concept takes us back to the times of the early church. Holistic mission encompassed worship and proclamation, public witness and service, transformation, reconciliation, and empowerment. Today, how holistic mission is lived out differs significantly depending on context. What seems to be important, however, is a commitment to witness that is a balance of both word and deed.

For both Anglicans and Lutherans, and indeed for all churches engaged in ecumenical dialogue, there has been an inevitable expanding of our common

---

5. The Lutheran World Federation, *Mission in Context: Transformation. Reconciliation. Empowerment*, ed. Jack Messenger (Geneva: Lutheran World Federation Department for Mission and Development, 2004), 30.

understanding of the nature and mission of the church. Dialogue has also had the result of making clearer the nexus between the mission and unity of the church. As European Anglicans and Lutherans said to one another:

> Living in *koinonia* the Church does not exist by itself and for itself. It is not a self-sufficient island. Rather, it is called to worship and praise God and to bring before him all the joys, sufferings and hopes of humankind. It is sent into the world to continue Christ's loving service and to witness to his active presence among all people. It is an instrument for proclaiming and manifesting God's sovereign rule and saving grace.[6]

Anglican-Lutheran dialogue underscores the connection between partnership and mission. Because ecumenical dialogues work across many languages, theologians often refer to Greek New Testament terminology for the sake of clarity and precision. Thus, along with *koinonia*, *diakonia* refers to service, *martyria* to witness, and *leiturgia* to worship. In their common understanding of the Eucharist, Anglicans and Lutherans affirm its fruits in the "building up of the community of the Church and in the strengthening of faith and hope and of witness and service in daily life."[7] As the Hanover Report challenges both Anglicans and Lutherans:

> The eucharistic assembly as *koinonia* participates in and manifests the *leitourgia*, *martyria*, and *diakonia* of the Christ who is present to it and through it. It is in the eucharistic assembly that the church receives its identity (body of Christ) and its mission (to be offered for one another and for the world; 1 Cor. 10:16–17; 1 Cor. 11:17–26).

---

6. Anglican-Lutheran European Regional Commission, *Anglican-Lutheran Dialogue: The Report of the Anglican-Lutheran European Regional Commission, Helsinki, August–September 1982* (London: SPCK, 1983), #50 (hereafter cited as *Helsinki*). See also *Report of the Anglican-Lutheran International Conversations 1970–1972* (hereafter cited as *Pullach*, #59–60, in *Anglican-Lutheran Agreements, Regional and International 1972–2002* (Geneva: LWF, 2004), 31–32.
7. See *Helsinki*, #28.

In gathering, Word, prayer, meal, and sending the church is called and embraced by Christ for his mission and ministry in the world.[8]

As the Jerusalem Report on *diakonia* and the life of the church proclaims in vivid imagery:

> The Church gathered and the Church sent out to serve are like a river and a lake: there is a rhythm of flowing in, gathering for fellowship, teaching and sacrament, then gushing out to serve the world. *Koinonia* and *diakonia* reinforce each other. Both Anglicans and Lutherans understand that *diakonia* is not just about transforming the world but about being transformed themselves.[9]

Our shared theological reflections on mission, communion, and service empower the churches of both the Anglican Communion and the LWF to receive each other and also enable us to engage one another in fresh ways. At the global communion level this has meant that our work for mission (witness, justice and peace, advocacy, relief, and development) intrinsically expresses a fuller, biblical vision of what it means to be a communion of churches. The ecumenical vision of communion and mission gives a profound ecclesiological significance to the work of the Anglican Alliance and to the Department for World Service of the LWF. When the Anglican Alliance and the Department for World Service work together, as well as with the Roman Catholic agency Caritas, the World Council of Churches, and other Christian World Communions, such "partnerships in vision" are expressions of the profound communion that we share in mission. Even while we work and pray that we may be one, as the Lord Jesus and the Father are one, when we engage in mission together, we proclaim in action what we believe about

---

8. *The Diaconate as Ecumenical Opportunity: The Hanover Report of the Anglican-Lutheran International Commission,* in *Anglican-Lutheran Agreements, Regional and International 1972–2002* (Geneva: LWF, 2004); see also #19, ##20–28.

9. *To Love and Serve the Lord: Diakonia in the Life of the Church.* The Jerusalem Report of the Anglican-Lutheran International Commission (ALIC III) (Geneva: LWF, 2012), 20.

the church as communion:[10] "Communion, whose source is the very life of the Holy Trinity, is both the gift by which the Church lives and, at the same time, the gift that God calls the Church to offer to a wounded and divided humanity in hope of reconciliation and healing."[11]

Hearing the Spirit

Communion Across Difference in Ecumenical Dialogues

Ecumenical listening, both bilateral and multilateral, helps to deepen and strengthen the understanding of the principle of "unity in diversity" used so frequently in ecumenical circles. It is a simple truth that through listening and learning to know "the other," our own self-reflection is enhanced. We find ourselves reflecting on questions that so far might have seemed to be rather peripheral to us, yet were set into a new light through a different perspective from a sister church. This is the enrichment brought by the diversity of gifts granted by the Holy Spirit. Yet truly enriching ecumenical encounters do not halt at diversity but lead us to *koinonia*, to God-given communion.

One of the great ironies of the present age in the life of the church is that while so many of the church-dividing issues inherited from the fifth, eleventh, and sixteenth centuries have been resolved by the multilateral and bilateral ecumenical dialogues, many new church-dividing issues have arisen. The new issues revolve in one way or another around gender, marriage, family, and human sexuality. They are expressed in disagreement over the ordination or nonordination of women, divorce and remarriage, polygamy, artificial contraception, and the place of gay, lesbian, bisexual, and transgendered people in the life of the church. While these new series of issues and underlying questions perpetuate and exacerbate historic differences *between* churches, responses to them have created new kinds of local, regional, and

---

10. *The Church: Towards a Common Vision* §1, *Faith and Order Paper No. 214* (Geneva: WCC, 2013), 5 (hereafter cited as *TCTCV*).
11. *TCTCV* §1, 5.

global divisions *within* the churches. This has been the recent experience of the Anglican Communion, the LWF, and other global communions of churches. After so much dialogue and listening to one another, we are learning to listen to the Holy Spirit again!

Our disagreements on these issues point beyond themselves to underlying and unreconciled diversities in biblical hermeneutics, ecclesial processes of moral discernment, theological anthropology, and differing attitudes toward inculturation. They also point to unexamined questions of basic ecclesiology. The questions below remain current in ecumenical dialogues. How do you answer them?

Questions for Reflection

5. What does it mean to be a communion (*koinonia*) of churches?
6. What does communion itself mean? What is its source? What are its limits?
7. What are the relationships between *koinonia*, mission, and *diakonia* in your experience?
8. What are the various understandings and exercise of authority in the church? Who exercises such authority?

The Anglican Communion and the LWF both experience strain in the relationships between their member churches. Both global communions have undertaken different processes to understand and safeguard *koinonia* and mission. The two texts that exemplify such efforts are *The Anglican Communion Covenant* (2010) and *The Self-Understanding of the Lutheran Communion* (2015). The Anglican Communion and the LWF, despite strong similarities, created very different texts. Although written only five years apart, the two texts were created by two geographically and demographically similar global communions of churches engaged by the same bilateral and multilateral ecumenical dialogue partners. The *Covenant* seeks to be a binding text on its member churches while the Lutheran *Self-Understanding* text is a study document that seeks to engage its member churches on a process of theological and ecclesiological self-reflection.

Oddly, the Anglican *Covenant* reads like the legal basis of a federation or an alliance, while the Lutheran *Self-Understanding* seeks to identify and respond to the LWF as a communion of churches, rather than as a federation. The *Covenant* seeks affirmation on a series of common characteristics—shared with other traditions—in terms of foundational faith and order, mission, governance, and dispute resolution. By contrast, *Self-Understanding* sets out a series of "resources" for discerning a response to engage disagreements in critical and constructive ways. The "resources" are a series of identified shared theological convictions. These include the convictions that the gospel is the core of life in communion; that the word and sacrament are events of communion; that the message of the cross heals our brokenness; that the word of God creates and affirms both unity and diversity; and that the gospel entails freedom, respect, and bearing with one another. Each of these theological convictions is accompanied by questions for deeper reflection.[12]

Anglicans have much to receive from Lutherans about how they might also envision, articulate, and receive a robust vision of the gracious gift of God's communion, irreversibly restored in the paschal mystery of Christ, to which the church is called to be the sign and servant.[13] From the Lutheran perspective, an inspiring Anglican reflection on communion in the context of internal conflict is the 2008 text of the Inter-Anglican Theological and Doctrinal Commission, *Communion, Conflict and Hope*.[14] Lutherans admire the frank and honest study of communion within the painful internal Anglican reflection on strained communion surrounding debates on human sexuality. This hope-filled affirmation of God's gift of communion arising from a global contextual study process—an "ecclesiology from below"— provides a concrete model to Lutheran and other global communions. That

---

12. The Lutheran World Federation, *The Self-Understanding of the Lutheran Communion: A Study Document* (Geneva: LWF, 2015), 15–24.

13. *TCTCV*, §§25–27.

14. Inter-Anglican Theological and Doctrinal Commission, *Communion, Conflict and Hope: The Kuala Lumpur Report of the Third Inter-Anglican Theological and Doctrinal Commission* (London: Anglican Communion Office, 2008).

Communion, Conflict and Hope is apparently so little known in the Anglican Communion baffles the Lutheran coauthor of this chapter!

In the contemporary context, the ecumenical dialogues have shifted their agenda away from the historic church-dividing issues from the past to respond to changing circumstances and new contexts. For instance, the multilateral Commission on Faith and Order has recently undertaken careful reflections in the area of biblical hermeneutics, sources of authority, moral discernment in the churches, and, most importantly, ecclesiology: what do we believe about the communion and mission of the church that could justify its divisions? The bilateral dialogues of both the Anglican Communion and the LWF with their various dialogue partners explore many of these areas. The nature of salvation is an area of particular interest around the five hundredth anniversary of the Reformation. The Anglican Communion has addressed questions around salvation and the church with both the LWF and the Catholic Church. Lutherans have dialogued with Roman Catholics, resulting in a groundbreaking common statement, the *Joint Declaration on the Doctrine of Justification* (JDDJ). In the JDDJ, signed in 1999, Lutherans and Roman Catholics effectively overcame the fundamental church-dividing doctrinal question of the Reformation. In 2006 the World Methodist Council (WMC) became a signatory of the JDDJ, followed by the World Communion of Reformed Churches (WCRC) in 2017.

After years of study and reflection on the JDDJ, the Anglican Consultative Council (ACC) at its 2016 meeting in Lusaka, Zambia, formally "welcomed and affirmed the substance" of the JDDJ. At Westminster Abbey on October 31, 2017, the archbishop of Canterbury presented signed copies of the ACC-16 resolution to representatives of the Catholic Church and the LWF, in the presence of the leadership of the WMC and the WCRC. Since 2018, the five global communions that have formally adhered to the JDDJ have engaged one another in a new kind of multilateral dialogue that seeks to discern the implications of their common adherence to the JDDJ in communion, witness, and mission. The place of the JDDJ within the history of the ecumenical movement is significant for at least three reasons. First, it shows that a seemingly intractable church-dividing issue is open to resolution. Moreover, such theological resolutions can open new ways of being churches together. Second, the kind of agreement achieved in the JDDJ is identified as a "differentiated consensus," which means a consensus on essential truths while admitting remaining differences or differing explications. Here is a theological unity in diversity. Third, it shows that agreement reached between two dialogue partners may be received more broadly.

Recent ecumenical dialogues have also addressed other kinds of issues that have arisen in our histories of division and have sought deeper unity through the healing of memories. Anglicans note in particular the action of the LWF toward the Mennonite World Conference in 2010. From the sixteenth century, other churches systematically persecuted the smaller Mennonite and other Anabaptist communities regarded as part of the "Radical Reformation." Over the centuries, this experience of intra-Christian persecution became one of the unhealed memories of the Reformation. After years of dialogue and study together, the 2010 agreed statement *Healing Memories: Reconciling in Christ. Report of the Lutheran-Mennonite International Study Commission* was published. The global Lutheran Communion took the unprecedented action of acknowledging its past violence against the ancestors of modern Mennonites and sought forgiveness and reconciliation. The "Mennonite Action" was celebrated in the context of the liturgical celebration at the 11th LWF Assembly in 2010. The Anglican Communion also took note of the initiative of the Lutheran-Roman Catholic Commission on Unity around the healing of memories in the context of the 2017 commemoration of the five hundredth anniversary of the Reformation, and the fiftieth anniversary of dialogue between Lutherans and Catholics. In the 2012 agreed statement *From Conflict to Communion: Lutheran-Catholic Common Commemoration of the Reformation in 2017*, Lutherans and Roman Catholics discovered that they could now tell the story of the events of the Reformation together in a way that opens up the possibility of a common future. The joint Lutheran-Roman Catholic gathering in Lund, Sweden, marking the beginning of the Reformation anniversary year on October 31, 2016, was a sign of this common future. Pope Francis and representatives of the Roman Catholic community gathered with Lutheran leaders and representatives to mark the anniversary together within the context of a broad ecumenical gathering.

These two initiatives between the LWF and its bilateral dialogue partners are significant for at least four reasons. First, they remind us that divisions are historical, and that corporate memories of division and violent behavior toward one another require a healing of ecclesial memories. Second, the reception of *Healing Memories* took place in the context of an act of worship, repentance, and reconciliation between the LWF and the Mennonite World Conference in the presence of the wider ecumenical family. Similarly, the reception of *From Conflict to Communion* took place in an act of worship on October 31, 2016, that included Pope Francis. Third, in the course of that celebration, two of the largest church-based agencies for relief and development—Lutheran World Service and Caritas International—entered into a concordat with one another. Here, a theological agreement that was received publicly and liturgically included a commitment to common mission. Fourth, as a result of these two bilateral relationships, a third emerged, namely a trilateral dialogue on baptism with Lutheran, Roman Catholic, and Mennonite partners.

A new feature of the current ecumenical time for the churches of the Anglican Communion, the LWF, and their common dialogue partners is the emergence of an entirely new ecumenical methodology called *receptive ecumenism*. Emerging from the United Kingdom in the early 2000s, receptive ecumenism quickly became a global phenomenon. Itself a response to the slow reception of the ecumenical dialogues and the newer church-dividing questions, receptive ecumenism starts from the premise that no single church on its own possesses the truth in faith and praxis. In order to grow into the church to which Christ calls us, we need to learn from one another. It is not about one church offering its insights and "best practices" to another church. Rather, it begins within a church asking itself, in humble honesty, where a weakness or shortcoming in its own life, faith, and mission could be strengthened and healed by something in the life of another church. By receiving something into its life from another Christian community, not only is one church blessed and renewed but the churches draw closer together in communion, even where ecumenical dialogue is slow or new church-dividing issues have emerged.

Processes of receptive ecumenism can be undertaken at the local, regional, and international levels and have even been employed in a bilateral theological dialogue. The Anglican-Roman Catholic International Commission (ARCIC) employed such a methodology in its 2017 agreed statement, *Walking Together on the Way: Learning to Be the Church—Local, Regional, Universal*. The text looks at ecclesial life in both communions at the local, regional, and global levels; members of both traditions pose to their respective churches where they identify something in the life of the other that needs to be appropriately received into their ecclesial life for the renewal and unity of the church. *Walking Together* is also an ecclesiological text that explores how differences in ecclesiology affect structures of decision-making.

At the global level of the LWF, Anglicans might well identify instances of governance that would strengthen its so-called Instruments of Communion. How could the ACC receive from the LWF its constitutional insistence on a certain percentage of youth and seniors, women and men, lay and ordained within its life? As the Anglican Communion seeks to assess the missiological and ecclesiological significance of the Anglican Alliance—its only global instrument for advocacy, relief, and development—what can it learn from the LWF priorities around its department for world service? As the Anglican Communion's communication strategy struggles to go beyond the English language, what can be learned from the multilingual capacities of the LWF's Office for Communication?

Ecumenical Friendship

One of the things that we have learned from an ecclesiology of communion is the role of friendship. A communion or *koinonia* of friendship exists between friends of different Christian traditions and within interchurch families, ecumenical schools, monastic communities, and organizations. We

may not always appreciate the ecclesiological, ecumenical, or theological significance of such friendships as expressing the true nature of the church as
the community of the friends of Jesus. We may not always see the strategic
value of friendship as a response to Jesus's prayer to the Father that we may
be one. Yet friendship is intrinsic to the life of the churches' bilateral and
multilateral dialogues. From our combined experience we can affirm that
the most successful ecumenical dialogues are those in which total strangers have become lifelong friends and learned to bear each other's joys and
sorrows. In the laboratory context of an ecumenical dialogue, friendships
between individuals and church bodies are as important as any text that
is produced. Indeed, such experiences point to the deep ecclesial nature of
friendship (John 15:15–17).

One of the authors of this chapter is John, from the Anglican Church
of Canada. For him, the Canadian Anglican experience of growing into full
communion with the Evangelical Lutheran Church in Canada is a compelling example of ecumenical friendship. John remembers well the years spent
in the 1980s and 1990s when theological dialogue between Lutherans and
Anglicans brought them closer together. These were also years of crisis for the
Anglican Church of Canada. It was during this time that the scandal of abuse
that took place in its residential schools for First Nations children became public. Canadian Anglicans, and members of other churches who had participated
in the residential schools created by the federal government in the late nineteenth century, were shamed. By the 1990s, the General Synod of the Anglican
Church of Canada faced the possibility of bankruptcy due to lawsuits. The
very public nature of this disgraceful history, combined with the real possibility
of the Anglican Church of Canada disappearing as a legal entity, did not make
them an attractive ecumenical partner for full communion. The reaction of the
Evangelical Lutheran Church in Canada was not, however, to delay or avoid
a full communion relationship with Anglicans. Quite the contrary, Lutherans
said to their Anglican sisters and brothers that even if the Anglican Church of
Canada were to become bankrupt, they still wanted to be in full communion
with them. Moreover, in the case that the Anglicans lost their church buildings,

Lutherans said that their churches would be Anglican churches. Of equal significance, Canadian Lutherans additionally took on the responsibilities of reconciliation with First Nations, even though they were never associated with the residential school system. Lutherans were also diligent about educating their people and engaging in practices such as land acknowledgment.

In the years leading to the Waterloo Agreement and establishing full communion between the two churches, not all Anglicans were in favor. Some were indifferent or hesitant. Some saw the agreement as ecumenically anomalous. The offer of costly ecumenical friendship offered by the Evangelical Lutheran Church to the Anglican Church of Canada in a time of crisis, however, won over Anglican hearts and minds. The Waterloo Agreement was duly approved by both churches in 2001. The success of Waterloo was not simply its maturity as a text, or the careful steps taken by both churches to get there. It was successful because of the care and generosity shown by Canadian Lutherans toward Anglicans in their hour of need. The federal government stepped in and the bankrupting lawsuit did not take place. But the friendship of the Lutherans was remembered.

The other author of this chapter is Anne, who is from the Estonian Evangelical Lutheran Church. Having attended high school and university in Estonia during the times of major transitions in society, she was the first one in her family to become a Christian after an interruption of one generation. The time when she started to attend the church more intensely overlapped with the time of the Porvoo agreement. Thus, for her, the fact that the Lutheran Church in Estonia was in full communion with several Anglican churches in the British Isles was already a given fact when she started her studies in 1994. First attempts to establish communion between the Church of England and the Baltic Lutheran Churches had already taken place in the 1930s. The interruption of the Soviet era put such connections "on hold." Indeed, they were largely forgotten by regular churchgoers. After Estonia regained its independence, the Lutheran Church started to open up and broaden their connections abroad. Several partnerships were formed, especially with the Finnish,

Swedish, and German Lutheran churches. The timing of Porvoo added Anglican churches to these interchurch relationships, bringing the Estonian Lutheran Church again into a deeper fellowship not only with the broader Lutheran family but also with Anglicanism.

Porvoo has had a clear impact on the Estonian Evangelical Lutheran Church. Especially in the late 1990s to the early 2000s, it intensified discussions about ecclesiology and ministry and strengthened the consciousness of the principle of "unity in diversity." However, while there seem to be many contacts on the level of church government, and especially from the representatives of the Church of England Diocese of Rochester—a partner diocese, who are always invited to the annual clergy conferences of the Estonian Evangelical Lutheran Church—there is still some room for improvement in the area of deepening partnerships between congregations. This is essential in order to make sure that Porvoo does not remain an agreement that is real only for theologians and clergy.

The authors of this chapter are friends. They have worked together on global Anglican-Lutheran relations—one at the Anglican Communion Office and the other at the Communion Office of the LWF. The likelihood that an English-speaking Canadian Anglican, born in the late 1950s, and an Estonian Lutheran, born in the 1970s under Soviet occupation, could ever have become colleagues and friends can only be explained by the richness and dynamism of the ecumenical movement. More specifically, it can only be explained by the *koinonia* found in the world of Anglican and Lutheran ecumenism.

Mission, communion, and Christian unity are linked historically, theologically, and pastorally. This connection is inextricable. The ecumenical question of Christian disunity was first raised by missionaries in the early twentieth century. They experienced a distorted proclamation of the gospel because of Christian disunity. A recovered theological appreciation for the New Testament understanding of communion as *koinonia* has practical consequences for how we understand disunity and unity, the mission of God (*missio Dei*), and the mission of the church.

Communion, whose source is the very life of the Holy Trinity, is both the gift by which the Church lives and, at the same time, the gift that God calls the Church to offer to a wounded and divided humanity in hope of reconciliation and healing.[15]

The churches of the Anglican Communion and the Lutheran World Federation have both contributed to and been shaped by this vision in the dialogues and encounters with one another and with common ecumenical partners. The challenges of strained communion that we have experienced in the wider ecumenical context are similar to those that we face within our particular communions of churches at this time. The theological questions about the nature and purpose of the church and the practical questions of communion and mission are one. As Anglicans and Lutherans reflect on our past achievements of deepening communion and common mission with one another, and within the wider ecumenical context, we are filled with hope for the work ahead.

Questions for Reflection

9. How might you learn about the different Christian churches in your context? Why not visit some of them?

10. To what extent is the week of prayer for Christian unity taken seriously in your context? What can you do to encourage regular prayer for the unity of the church during this week and at other times?

11. With which churches is your own church in ecumenical dialogue? If you do not know the answer, how might you find it?

12. Try to imagine how the churches working together where you live could make a difference toward justice and peace. Make a list of the possibilities. As you reflect on this chapter, say aloud the following prayer:

Almighty God,
you have knit your people together

---

15. *TCTCV*, §1.

in one communion in the mystical body of your Son, Jesus
    Christ our Lord.

Grant us grace to follow your saints in lives of faith and
    commitment,

and to know the inexpressible joys you have prepared for those
    who love you,

through Jesus Christ, our Savior and Lord,

who lives and reigns with you and the Holy Spirit, one God,
    now and forever.

Amen.[16]

---

16. The Collect for All Saints Day, *Evangelical Lutheran Worship* (Canada & USA, 2006).

8

Communion and Interreligious Questions

Clare Amos and Daniel Sperber

With the possible exception of the Book of Common Prayer Good Friday Collect asking God to have "mercy upon all Jews, Turks,[1] Infidels and Hereticks, and take from them all ignorance, hardness of heart, and contempt of thy word,"[2] the first reference to other religions in official Anglican documents comes in the resolutions of the 1897 Lambeth Conference. There are three resolutions from that conference that specifically relate to "other religions."

Resolution 15

That the tendency of many English-speaking Christians to entertain an exaggerated opinion of the excellences of Hinduism and Buddhism, and to ignore the fact that Jesus Christ alone has been constituted Saviour and King of mankind, should be vigorously corrected.

Resolution 16

That a more prominent position be assigned to the evangelisation of the Jews in the intercessions and almsgiving of the Church. . . .

---

1. In the seventeenth century the word "Turk" was used as a synonym for "Muslim."
2. The 1662 Book of Common Prayer, the Society of Archbishop Justus, http://justus.anglican.org/resources/bcp/1662/collects.pdf.

Resolution 17

That in view:

1. of the success which has already attended faithful work among
   the Mohammedans [*sic*],
2. of the opportunity offered at the present time for more vigorous
   efforts, especially in India and in the Hausa district and
3. of the need of special training for the work, it is desirable:
   a. that men be urged to offer themselves with a view to preparation
      by special study for mission work among Mohammedans;
   b. that attention be called to the importance of creating or maintaining
      strong centres for work amongst Mohammedans. . . .

Although not entirely negative about adherents of other religions, these resolutions see them as targets for evangelism and conversion rather than dialogue
and cooperation. Resolution 14 specifically commends "missionary zeal" and
reminds its readers of the need for the "fulfilment of our Lord's great commission to evangelise all nations."

It is interesting to wonder why "other religions" should suddenly make
an appearance at the Lambeth Conference. Is it connected with the first
gathering of the Parliament of Religions in Chicago in 1893, and the varied
Anglican reactions to it? The archbishop of Canterbury at the time, Edward
Benson, when asked to send his good wishes to the meeting, refused, commenting: "The Christian religion is the one religion. I do not understand
how that religion can be regarded as a member of a Parliament of Religions
without assuming the equality of the other intended members and the parity
of their position and claims."[3] Despite this, most of the bishops of what was
then called "the Protestant Episcopal Church of America" were positive about
the event, and several took part in its organization. Presumably the excitement

---

3. Quoted in John Henry Barrows, *The World's Parliament of Religions: An Illustrated
and Popular Story of the World's First Parliament of Religions, Held in Chicago in
Connection with the Columbian Exposition of 1893,* vol. 1 (Charleston, SC: Nabu
Press, 2010), 20–21.

caused by the establishment of the Parliament and the varied reactions to it may have been a reason why "other religions" made it onto the agenda of the Lambeth Conference four years later, even if only to be firmly put in their place! With one exception (see below), "other religions" did not feature again in the Lambeth Conference resolutions for another seventy years, until 1968, when developments in the Roman Catholic Church and at the World Council of Churches led to an explicit and positive affirmation of interreligious dialogue.[4] Given the emphasis on relations with other churches that runs through most of the Lambeth Conferences of this period, the absence of attention to other religions becomes even more marked. Since 1968, the issue of interreligious dialogue has been on the agenda of every Lambeth Conference. It was given particular attention in 1978, when the report "The Way of Dialogue" was affirmed, and in 2008 when the report "Generous Love: The Truth of the Gospel and the Call to Dialogue" was discussed.[5] The exception is the 1948 Lambeth Conference, where there is a resolution that names Jews and Muslims in a very specific context. The resolution reads:

Resolution 16: The Church and the Modern World—Palestine

The Conference feels deep concern for the future of Palestine: it prays that good order and peace may be restored to the land sacred to millions of Christians as well as to Muslims and Jews. It greatly appreciates the efforts made to restore peace and expresses its sympathy with all of every race, and particularly Christians of every Church, who are suffering.

---

4. Relations with named "other religions" were part of the discussion at the Pan-Anglican Congress, which took place just before the Lambeth Conference of 1908. They were, however, still seen primarily as a target for evangelism and conversion.
5. There were no resolutions passed at the 2008 Lambeth Conference, so although "Generous Love" was discussed and largely appreciated, it was not formally commended. See Anglican Communion "Generous Love: The Truth of the Gospel and the Call to Dialogue," accessed August 15, 2019, https://nifcon.anglicancommunion .org/interactive/_books/default.asp#page0.

The Conference appeals to the nations of the world to deal with the problem [not as one of expediency—political, strategic, or economic—but as a moral] and spiritual question that touches a nerve centre of the world's religious life. And for that reason it urges the United Nations to place Jerusalem and its immediate environs under permanent international control, with freedom of access to sacred places secured for the adherents of the three religions.[6]

Clearly the focus is on the well-being of Christians, especially Palestinian Christians, but at least Muslims and Jews are referred to in a way that moves beyond seeing them as targets for conversion, and acknowledges the importance of Jerusalem for both Judaism and Islam as well as Christianity. There is, however, no direct reference to the possibility of dialogue with their adherents. Indeed, rereading the material of the 1948 Lambeth Conference seventy years afterward it seems strange that there was no resolution which spoke about the horrors of the Holocaust and the topic of Christian antisemitism.[7] Presumably the more immediate problems in Israel/Palestine took precedence. The importance of Jerusalem is a consistent theme in Anglican interreligious relations—a topic we will return to below.

In 2015 Clare Amos and Michael Ipgrave cowrote the chapter on Anglican interreligious dialogue and engagement for the *Oxford Handbook of Anglican Studies*. Part of the thesis was that as far as official Anglican structures were concerned, there was an inherent untidiness when it came to locating "interreligious dialogue." Did it fit with "mission," "ecumenism," or "social responsibility"? One can find examples of Anglican structures that reflect each understanding. Amos and Ipgrave concluded that in reality it was linked to all

6. The Lambeth Conference, "Resolutions Archive from 1948," Anglican Communion Office, 2005, https://www.anglicancommunion.org/media/127737/1948.pdf.
7. This contrasts with the first World Council of Churches General Assembly that took place in the same year and in which a forceful critique of antisemitism was expressed. It was referred to as "sin against God and man." See World Council of Churches, "WCC Policy on Palestine and Israel 1948–2016 (Summary)," January 1, 2017, https://www.oikoumene.org/en/resources/documents/wcc-programmes/public-witness/peace-building-cf/wcc-policy-on-palestine-and-israel-1948-2016-summary.

three—and that is ultimately one of the principles of Anglican interreligious engagement. Such engagement must inform Anglican understandings of mission and partnership. Ninian Smart sets out ten theses that he believed the Anglican tradition could offer to the dialogue of religions. His tenth thesis reads, "Anglicanism, as chaotic and incompetent, is ready to be diffident, and so can avoid arrogance in regard to other faiths."[8] Perhaps that structural untidiness—in which interreligious dialogue overlaps with mission, ecumenism, and social responsibility—is part of the Anglican contribution to wider interreligious work.

One of the insights Ipgrave and Amos offered is that there are significant connections between mission and interreligious dialogue. We use the word *mission* here in its narrow sense (evangelism and conversion) as well as in its wider sense (the mission of God). Many Anglican pioneers in interreligious dialogue and engagement began their interest through going as missionaries to parts of Africa, Asia, and the Middle East. As they grew to love the places and people where they served, they came to appreciate that the call to witness to Christ might be appropriately achieved through hospitality and dialogue rather than deliberately seeking explicit conversions from other faiths. This pattern goes back into the early nineteenth century—well before the 1897 Lambeth Conference. Indeed, Resolution 15 of that conference may be directed at missionaries in, for example, India who had come to appreciate the need for mutual dialogue with Hindus and Buddhists. It is a pattern that formed part of Anglican realities for much of the twentieth century. Perhaps its classic exemplar is Bishop Kenneth Cragg (1913–2012), who for decades was a world-famous exponent of dialogue between Christians and Muslims, and whose study of Islam, *The Call of the Minaret* (1956), remains a classic. Cragg played a considerable role in encouraging the developing interest in interreligious relations at the World Council of Churches, which in turn influenced the deliberations of the 1968 Lambeth Conference. Eventually, in

---

8. Ninian Smart, "The Anglican Contribution to the Dialogue of Religions," *Theology* (July 1967): 302–9.

1994, Anglicans would establish the Network for Inter Faith Concerns of the Anglican Communion (NIFCON).

This "missionary bridge" into interreligious dialogue is captured well in a set of books published in the 1950s and 1960s called the Christian Presence series, largely authored by Anglicans. The series editor, Max Warren, had been general secretary of the Church Missionary Society. The best-known books in the series were written by Kenneth Cragg (*Sandals at the Mosque*) and John V. Taylor (*The Primal Vision*). A paragraph in Warren's series introduction captures the spirit of what is meant by "presence":

> Our first task in approaching another people, another culture, another religion, is to take off our shoes, for the place we are approaching is holy. Else we may find ourselves treading on men's dreams. More serious still, we may forget that God was here before our arrival. We have, then, to ask what is the authentic religious content in the experience of the Muslim, the Hindu, the Buddhist, or whoever he may be. We may, if we have asked humbly and respectfully, still reach the conclusion that our brothers have started from a false premise and reached a faulty conclusion. But we must not arrive at our judgement from outside their religious situation. We have to try to sit where they sit, to enter sympathetically into their pains and griefs and joys of their history and see how those pains and griefs and joys have determined the premises of their argument. We have, in a word, to be "present" with them.[9]

This short passage captures what has become the classic Anglican understanding regarding engagement with other religions.[10]

---

9. John V. Taylor, introduction to *The Primal Vision* (London: SCM Press, 1963), 10–11.
10. Expressed, for example, in the report "Generous Love."

Hearing Scripture

As we shall explore, "presence" requires space, and "holy space" is both important and contested in the texts and contexts of the religions of the world.

Unlike most of the other contributors to this volume, we do not share the same religion. Nor do we exactly share the same scriptures. We first met through the regular formal meetings for dialogue that the Anglican Communion has held with the chief rabbinate of Israel since 2006, being members of our respective delegations.[11] We both accept that though superficially the Hebrew Bible and the Old Testament may appear to be the same document, they are actually different, partly because they are respectively linked to other and different scriptures: the rabbinic writings for Judaism and the New Testament for Christianity. They are also different in themselves, since the canonical shape of the Christian Old Testament (ending with Malachi) conveys a different message from the canonical shape of the Hebrew Bible (ending with 2 Chronicles). We are deliberately, therefore, not offering a common Bible study. Amos offers a Bible study from a Christian perspective on two psalms and Sperber's reflection discusses the related theme of "holiness" from a Jewish perspective. It is no accident that the theme we have both chosen to reflect on centers on the importance of Jerusalem. This has been an important topic in our ongoing dialogue. It links to the theme of "presence," which, as suggested above, is a characteristic insight vital to Anglican approaches to other religions. It is also reflective of the importance that the Holy Land has had in Anglican thinking about dialogue and mission.

There are many texts in the Old Testament/Hebrew Bible, as well as in the New Testament, which focus on Jerusalem. Amos's chosen scriptural entry-point is Psalms 48 and 87, both of which express the importance of Jerusalem. Although the two psalms come from different "books" of the Psalter, and may have been composed at different periods of Israel's (or Judah's) history,

---

11. See https://nifcon.anglicancommunion.org/media/111580/Agreement-between-The-Chief-Rabbis-of-Israel-and-The-Archbishop-of-Canterbury.pdf, accessed October 29, 2019.

they form part of the group of psalms (42–49; 82–89) linked to the "sons of Korah." The "sons of Korah" are described in 1 Chronicles 9:17–19 as "gatekeepers" and "guardians of the threshold" of the Jerusalem temple. These "Korah" psalms convey a sense of passion and longing for Jerusalem and worship in the temple.

Psalm 48 offers an unambiguous proclamation of God's protection of Jerusalem. It is God's own city. God will show himself a "sure defense." If enemies attack Jerusalem, they will be doomed to failure. It is interesting that in the psalm the word "Jerusalem" does not appear. The city is three times described as "Zion," which is probably the name of one of the hills on which Jerusalem was built. This name seems to be especially used in the scripture to which the strength and impregnability of the city is being alluded. The final verses of the psalm describe an "inspection visit" of the city. The people are encouraged to check out the city's defenses for themselves in the surety of God's eternal protection. Whatever the "kings" (here understood as God's enemies; see Ps. 2:2 and Rev. 21:24) may try, they will be doomed to ignominious failure. A striking "clue" to the theological meaning of the psalm is offered in the first and second verses:

> Great is the LORD and greatly to be praised
> in the city of our God.
> His holy mountain, beautiful in elevation,
> is the joy of all the earth,
> Mount Zion, in the far north,
> the city of the great King.

It is easy to hear these lines without initially realizing their strangeness. Zion/Jerusalem is described as "God's holy mountain, beautiful in elevation." However, the historical Mount Zion was not particularly impressive as a mountain. Whichever part of modern-day Jerusalem it was—whether the Temple Mount/Haram esh-Sharif or what is today called "the City of David"—in height it was overshadowed by the nearby Mount of Olives. Behind this description lies the biblical vision of a mountain as the place for divine-human encounter (obvious in the Sinai stories). The passion of the psalmist for God is reflected in the hyperbole with which God's mountain is described. This is even more apparent when we consider the puzzling description "in the far north." Mount Zion is not in the "far north"—unless viewed from the Southern Hemisphere! It is not even in the north of the kingdom of Judah or of Davidic/Solomonic Israel. If the description is referring to the Temple Mount/Haram esh-Sharif, it is north, just, of the rest of the city of Jerusalem. It is certainly not the "far north." The author is drawing upon wider cultural images and associations.

The discovery, in the 1930s, of the Ugaritic/Ras Shamra texts that describe the religious and cultural beliefs of the ancient city of Ugarit (in modern-day coastal Syria) helped elucidate what is behind these words. The texts tell of a high mountain a few miles north of the city that was considered the dwelling place of the Canaanite gods worshiped by the inhabitants of Ugarit. The mountain was called "Zaphon." This Hebrew/Canaanite word *zaphon* means "north" and was appropriate given the location of the mountain in relation to the city. These religious and cultural resonances are being recalled in the biblical psalm. The word *zaphon* seemingly alludes to Mount Zion as the place of divine dwelling, in this case of the God of Israel rather than of the deities worshipped at Ugarit. The *Common Worship* version of this psalm catches this well as it translates *zaphon*/north as "divine dwelling place": "On Mount Zion, the divine dwelling place, stands the city of the great king."[12]

This, then, is the fundamental reason that Jerusalem will be protected from any enemies—God himself dwells there. Divine presence acts as a guarantee of human security. The tale of pre-exilic and exilic Israel/Judah is a story of debate on this claim. It is an internal controversy within scripture itself. Over against psalms such as 48 (see also Ps. 50, 78, 84), which cherish such a "presence theology," stand the oracles of Jeremiah, who in his temple sermon (Jer. 7, 26), first mocks and then demolishes the idea that the temple will always protect the people from external danger. It seems that "presence

12. The Church of England, "Psalm 48," https://www.churchofengland.org/prayer-and-worship/worship-texts-and-resources/common-worship/common-material/psalter/psalm-48.

theology" gained extra credibility from events that took place during the reign of Hezekiah. In that time Jerusalem was miraculously delivered from a besieging Assyrian army. A hundred years or so later, this had hardened into the abusive attitudes that Jeremiah sought to counter.

Biblical texts from the period of the Babylonian exile wrestle with the apparent failure of "presence theology." The experiences of the conquered people seemed a sign that it was no longer valid. The exilic writers respond in a variety of ways. Ezekiel provides a particularly vivid and dramatic description of God leaving Jerusalem on his heavenly chariot to take refuge with the exiles in Babylon. This is intended, at least in part, as an explanation for the fall of Jerusalem. One of the most poignant examples of exilic writing includes an intertextual allusion to Psalm 48 (and Psalm 50). Lamentations 2:15 refers to people mocking the destroyed Jerusalem:

> All who pass along the way
> . . . hiss and wag their heads
> at daughter Jerusalem;
> "Is this the city that was called
> the perfection of beauty,
> the joy of all the earth?"

The phrase "The joy of all the earth" alludes back to Psalm 48:2 and is a bitter jeer at the theology underpinning the psalm.

Psalm 87 is also one linked to the "sons of Korah." Love for Jerusalem and the temple is gloriously apparent, as is well captured in the opening lines of the famous Christian hymn by John Newton, "Glorious things of thee are spoken, O city of God." Interpreting the psalm presents difficulties, however. It feels like a disconnected series of interjections from several different voices linked primarily by their passion for Jerusalem. It is not clear who is "I/me" and who is "you" in the psalm. Is it Jerusalem herself personified and speaking?

What is particularly remarkable is the list given of nations born in Zion: Rahab (probably a metaphor for Egypt), Babylon, Philistia, Tyre, and Ethiopia. These nations were notorious for their hostility to Israel. Here, it seems, they will still be welcomed and invited to "belong" to Jerusalem.

Psalm 87, like Psalm 48, has as its fundamental premise the belief that Jerusalem is the dwelling place of God. The conclusions drawn, however, are very different. In the one psalm the "presence theology" is a guarantee of national security. In the other, God's presence constitutes an invitation drawing even the most unlikely groups and nations to find a home in Jerusalem. What are the implications of these two similar—yet also contrasting—understandings of Jerusalem? What insights do they offer for mission? Perhaps the following can offer a basis for your reflection.

Our assurance of God's presence presents us with a challenge as to how we use it in our engagement and interaction with others. The New Testament picks up the biblical language of God dwelling in Jerusalem and transfers it to the person of Jesus Christ. According to the Gospel of John, God "dwells" in Jesus Christ rather than in the temple of Jerusalem (John 1:14). But whether we think of God's presence manifest in a city or in a human being, the question is similar: Do we see God's presence as something that we are privileged to possess and need to defend from others ("outsiders"), or do we see God's presence as essentially invitational? Is God drawing others in to share our joy and excitement? Of course, since we are exploring this theme with the aid of two psalms, questions raised about the nature of psalmody—our words to God, as much as God's words to us—cannot be ignored. If the Psalms are a "mirror to the soul"[13] and an invitation to conversation with God, then perhaps, in an almost sacramental way, "Jerusalem" forces us to face some hard questions about ourselves and our attitudes that we might prefer to keep politely hidden.

But there is also another issue that impinges upon the nature of mission itself. The Christian paradigm of mission has, certainly for the last two centuries, been seen as what we call "centrifugal." Mission was understood as a journeying out from a center to the peripheries. The concern was to carry the gospel into the world and to convert others to a Christian understanding of what faith in God means. This is a model that we can

---

13. The idiom of "mirror" in relation to the Psalms is used by several classic theologians, including Athanasius of Alexandria and John Calvin.

find in parts of the New Testament (Matt. 28:16–20; Luke 10:1–12), but this is not the whole biblical understanding of mission. Donald Senior and Carroll Stuhlmueller in *The Biblical Foundations for Mission* (1983) point to strands of mission that encourage "centripetal" movement: not a journey outward from a center but a journey *toward* a center. In this mode of thinking, the missionary task is primarily to shine like a light set on a hill, so that those who choose can find their way there and discover warmth and welcome. As Senior and Stuhlmueller note, it is particularly the parts of the Old Testament / Hebrew Bible such as the Psalms and Isaiah, in which Jerusalem is important, that present this alternative model of mission. It is expressed powerfully in the oracle of Isaiah 2:1–4 (paralleled in Micah 4:1–4). At its best, "presence theology" linked to Jerusalem can facilitate such a centripetal understanding.

The longing to "see the face of the Lord" in the temple of which many psalms sing so eloquently is an incentive to journey toward "the city set on a hill." Psalm 87 suggests this very model of mission in which people are invited to "come and see" and participate for themselves in the community of divine celebration. Here, it seems, is an inclusive and not forbidding community that invites pilgrimage and eschews defensiveness, harshness, and judgmentalism. What does such a model of mission mean for Anglican Christians?

Questions for Reflection

1. How do you understand the place of the Psalms in Christian (and Jewish) scripture? Can they be both our words to God and God's words to us? To what extent do you resonate with the description offered in the fourth century by St. Athanasius that they are "a picture, in which you see yourself portrayed, and seeing, may understand and consequently form yourself upon the pattern given"?

2. It has been said that all religion is a quest for the presence of God. To what extent do you think this is true? What have you learned about the theme of divine presence from your exploration of Psalms 48 and 87?

3. We have drawn attention to the way that the implications of a biblical theme—in this case the belief that God dwelt in Jerusalem—can be understood in a variety of ways and offer positive and negative challenges to us today. What challenges do these readings offer you?

4. The exegesis has drawn attention to the different directions of mission and suggested that there is a place for a "centripetal" understanding of mission. What would this mean in your context?

Hearing Each Other

Working together as Jewish and Christian scholars is a reminder that there are many fundamentals we share, including a love for the Psalms. Yet our different histories over the centuries and millennia have meant that the Psalms have been understood in diverse ways. As we have seen, these diverse understandings have implications for witness and mission. Indeed, the very word "mission" can be heard in different ways by Jews and Christians.

The five marks of mission make it clear that "mission," as Anglicans understand it, is multidimensional. Mission is more than evangelism. "Mission" is a word that is often understood by Christians in positive terms. However, for Jews it often carries with it a sense of threat and a reminder of periods when Christians tried forcibly to "convert" Jews to Christianity. While these days are past, inevitably Jews remain suspicious of Christians who seek to see Jews convert to Christianity. Given the vast global disparity between the numbers of Christians and Jews, such activities appear like the targeting of a vulnerable minority. It also begs questions about the genuine Christian understanding of Judaism as a living sister faith. As a Christian scholar and a Jewish scholar working together, for us these are issues that remain crucial. To what extent are Christians wedded to an understanding of mission and ministry as "expansion" into non-Christian space? This is a pertinent question when the non-Christians in view are Jewish and thus subscribe to a very particular understanding of "holy space."

Space in Jewish Understanding

When a religious person, from whichever religion, speaks of the sanctity of space, what does he or she mean? Is it something tangible or merely symbolic? Does he/she see it as something real?

Muslims remove their shoes when entering a mosque, as do Yemenite Jews when entering a synagogue. For them the space of the mosque or the synagogue is holy. Entering that space with shoes would desecrate the space. In some religions, one has to purify oneself before entering the "temple" area—for example, in some contemporary Islamic practices one purifies oneself by bathing in water or sprinkling oneself in holy water. A church is a place of sanctity that requires respect and respectful behavior such as, in some strands of Christianity, modest dress and covered heads. In contrast, Judaism possesses a whole structural theology of sanctity. From a Jewish perspective, though there is "awe" in a church, its sanctity is not tangible. The holiness is perceived as internal, in the faith of the worshiper, rather than in the space of the sanctuary.

Space has gradated degrees of holiness. In the temple itself there were various areas with different degrees of holiness. There was a general area into which anyone could come, provided that they were pure. Purity was connected to holiness. There were certain inner areas that were for special people (priests). There was also the innermost sanctum, which was called the holy of holies (*kodesh hakodashim*), that had the greatest intensity of holiness. The high priest alone would enter the holy of holies and only on the holiest day of the year (*Yom Ha-Kippurim*). These spatial gradations are paralleled by the gradations in the sanctity of time. Thus, when we speak of holy time, we distinguish between those festivals that have a lesser degree of sacredness and those which have a greater degree. In Judaism, the three so-called "foot festivals" are *Pesach* (Passover), *Shavuot* (Pentecost), and *Sukkot* (Tabernacles), and they seem to have a lesser degree of holiness compared to the Sabbath and *Yom Ha-Kippurim* (the Day of Awe). Thus, a festival could be a *yom kadosh* (a day of holiness) or it could be a day of extreme holiness.

There are also objects of holiness, again with a variety of different levels of sacredness. For instance, when we speak of sacrifices, they had at least two different degrees of holiness. There were those sacrifices that are called *kodashim kalim*, which literally means "light holiness," and had one set of rules, and those that are pure *kodashim,* which had a weightier degree of holiness and different rules. There were also various holy temple instruments, such as the altar, the golden altar of incense, the seven-branch candelabra, and the so-called Ark of the Law with its golden angels or seraphim on top. All these different categories that come under the generic category *kadosh*, *kedoshim,* or which have *kedushah* all have an inherent element of holiness. They remain holy even if a person cannot perceive their sacredness.

There are two different types of holiness. There is holiness which we invest in a place or an object, and there is holiness which is inherent, irrespective of any human relationship to it. When we build a synagogue or a church or a mosque or a temple, there is a process of investing it with sanctity. Moreover, the possibility exists to desanctify it should there be a need. Such need might arise when, for example, there has been a change in the demography of the population, when there has been a change in the political situation, or when the site (whether a field, cemetery, or sanctuary) is required for government use or for a government project. One time may require investing an object or place with sanctity and another time may require it to be desanctified. According to Jewish law, even sacred time is determined by the rabbis. It is the rabbis who decide the date of a certain festival and then that festival has the characteristics of sacred time.

The Sabbath was sanctified by God himself during the seven days of creation. Its sanctity is not dependent upon human action. There are other types within these categories that have an inherent sanctity which is not dependent upon human acts of sanctification, and which, according to most views in Jewish law, cannot be desanctified. According to tradition, the Temple Mount is one of the cardinal points of creation. Here, Adam was created; its sanctity is a God-invested sanctity and not a human-invested sanctity. Humans have no ability to desanctify such space.

When a person or a group of people sanctify a place, and grant it the temporality of sanctity, that place has sanctity. That sanctity is, as it were, dependent upon the continued relationship of people to it. In a sense, it is conditional. It does not mean that it is less holy, but its sanctity depends on certain ongoing factors. Thus, categories of conditional and unconditional sanctity exist and both have deep legal and practical implications for Jewish communities.

Hearing the Spirit

The Protection of Holy Space in Jewish Understanding

We have already explained how there is a gradation of intensities in sacredness. The classic source for this is the Mishnah (a collection of authoritative Jewish oral law). Probably from the first or second century of the Common Era, a section called *Keilim* (1:6) deals with the purities and impurities of objects and implements of various kinds. It states that there are ten different stages or degrees of holiness.

The degrees rise in intensity of holiness and begin with *Eretz Yisrael,* the Land of Israel, as the holiest of all lands. This does not imply that other lands are not holy, but it does mean that Israel is a holier land. Then there are walled cities, which are holier still within the holy land. Then within the walls of Jerusalem is an area called the *azarot,* which is even more holy. The area between those courtyards and the altar is holier still until we get to the tenth locus, which is the Holy of Holies (*kodesh kodashim*). This is the most holy place where the Ark of the Law (*Aron haBrit*) was to be found. It could only be entered once a year for a short time and for a particular ritual purpose carried out by the high priest.

How then does the Mishnah define these different types of holiness? It does not do so in spiritual terms, in any theological fashion, or in any philosophical expression. It does so in a strictly legal manner. It describes prohibitions or obligations associated with the sanctity of the land. Israel incurs a number of obligations that are not found in other lands, such as the giving of tithes and the giving of the first fruits, which are brought to Jerusalem. Within the walled cities there is a prohibition, a "haram," that a leper cannot live there. As we go further in, there are areas that only priests can enter and there are areas where one is obligated to bring sacrifices. Some of these sacrifices can be eaten by a layman in one sort of area and other sacrifices can only be eaten by priests in another area. At all stages of these ten different degrees of sanctity, the text describes legal obligations and prohibitions: what is commanded in one area and what is forbidden in other areas. Since there is a growing gravitas in each of these obligations or prohibitions, so too the degree of sanctity is thought to rise until we get to the *kodesh hakodashim*, the most holy place, the innermost sanctum, where the Ark of the Law is to be found.

What, then, of ideas and practices of shared areas of holiness? Obviously non-Jewish people, Gentiles, could live in the holy land of Israel. Non-Jewish people can enter into the holy walled cities. Non-Jews could even enter into a certain area on the Temple Mount. In the Istanbul Archaeology Museum, a famous archaeological find is on display that exemplifies the limits of shared areas of holiness. It is an inscription in the Greek language that reads, "So up to this point, Gentiles are permitted to enter, further than that they are not permitted to enter." This underlines a gradation not only of sanctity but also of *haramim* (prohibitions). Up to the areas where these prohibitions obtain, there are areas which may be shared. The reader might think that these ancient texts are anachronistic and cannot possibly be relevant to the present day. This, however, is not the case. They have practical implications, even in the present day, such as concerning the issue of *shemitah*, the sabbatical year.

For the great Jewish thinker Rav Kook (1865–1935), the first chief rabbi of Israel, the sanctity of the land of Israel is intrinsic and not dependent upon its population. Thus, even if there were no Jews in the land of Israel to keep the laws, the land would still keep its innate sanctity. This is illustrated by a fine homiletic comment in the name of Rav Kook. The Talmud (B. Ketubot 112b) relates that Rabbi Hiyya bar Gamda would roll around in the dust [of *Eretz Yisrael*]: "For your servants hold its stones dear, and have pity on its dust" (Ps. 102:14). This he did when he arrived from Babylonia to the land of Israel (*Eretz Yisrael*) probably in the early third century CE. However, the same source tells us that when Rabbi Abba arrived, he kissed the sterile stones (perhaps cliffs) of Akko. Rav Kook asked, "Why did he kiss the stones and not the life-giving soil like Rabbi Hiyya bar Gamda?" His answer was that some people come to *Eretz-Yisrael* in order to be able to carry out those special commands (*mitzvot*) that pertain specifically to the land of Israel. But others come to the land out of their desire to merit the experience of its *intrinsic* holiness without reference to the laws obtaining to the land. Thus, Rabbi Abba kissed those stones, though they be sterile and have no special rules relating to them. Here we see that there are two different ways of considering this notion of holy space in Jewish thought. There is the legalistic aspect and there is a certain theological, ideological, or philosophical aspect that draws upon a whole different source or set of sources found in the writings of medieval philosophers.

The theological aspect, signifying the innate sanctity of the land given to it by God, may be regarded as granting eternal sanctity. What is clear is that the summit, the crowning point of this sanctity, is Jerusalem. It is holy to Christianity, to Islam, as well as to Judaism. But each religion has its own reasons and sources for this sanctity, and its own understanding thereof. What, however, they all share is the absolute need to recognize and respect that sanctity. This returns us to the consideration, in an explicitly interreligious context, of how Christians can interpret the text in light of the varied ways in which sacredness is understood and promoted in Judaism.

Christian Interpretation in Light of Jewish Sacredness

In Christian exegetical tradition there have been four senses of scripture. A biblical text addresses us in terms of history, belief, action, and hope. A medieval verse, ascribed to the Franciscan biblical scholar Nicholas of Lyra (1270–1340), expresses this:

> The literal sense teaches the things done
> The allegorical sense, what you should believe
> The moral sense, what you should do
> The anagogical sense, where you are heading.

We can consider what has already been explored in relation to Psalm 48 as the "literal" or historical sense, although such categories do not fully fit a psalm, with its focus on worship. For even though we looked at the historical and geographical context of the psalm, relating it to the temple in Jerusalem, believing in God's particular care for Jerusalem and Zion is an article of faith rather than of history. Nonetheless, starting from this "literal" sense we will consider briefly what might be allegorical, moral, and anagogical readings of Psalm 48, and particularly the understanding of "Zion" expressed in the psalm.[14]

- The allegorical sense of Zion might be identified as the community of faith, the mystical or spiritual body of believers, the Church that gives Christians their sense of identity.
- The moral sense of Zion might be identified as the visible and tangible parish church, the focus of a congregation's confidence in their activities.
- The anagogical sense of Zion might be identified as the hopeful and challenging symbol of the kingdom, which in its fullness is yet to come.

The allegorical sense of Zion—linking the name to the community of faith and therefore the body of Christ—is a long-standing aspect of Christian spirituality. For example, Augustine of Hippo, exegeting Psalm 48, says of Zion, "This is our city, if we are members of the King, who is the head of the same city." So the physical city of Jerusalem becomes a powerful metaphor for the people among whom God's grace and love is to be found. Indeed, this "personalizing" interpretation predates Christianity, as the Greek Septuagint translation of Psalm 48:9 reworks the Hebrew text translated as "in the midst of your temple" into "in the midst of your people." There is a deep resonance among many Christians with such a view. It is expressed powerfully in

---

14. These remarks draw on the exegesis of Ps. 48 by Michael Ipgrave. See Michael Ipgrave and Guy Wilkinson, eds., "Encouraging Reading: Ten Old Testament Bible Studies for Presence and Engagement," Church of England, https://www.churchofengland.org/sites/default/files/2019-05/Encouraging_Reading.pdf, 81–89.

Christian hymnody and perhaps *par excellence* in Newton's work mentioned earlier. The entire first verse of "Glorious things of thee are spoken" is drawn from Psalm 48, Psalm 46, and Psalm 87.

The theme of God's protecting presence, which is so evident in Psalm 48, is readily interpreted by Christians in the light of their experience of their own physical church building. The building, then, is seen to have its own vocation at the heart of the community. This might be described as a moral, or action-oriented, interpretation of Psalm 48. "Encouraging Reading" explores the motif as follows:

> The church building is for [many Christians] the place where God is especially honoured as his name is remembered and his praises sung. It is a place which is to be loved and cared for by its congregation, as a sacramental sign of his presence. It is also, like a mountain, a visible feature of the landscape, seen in different ways by the faithful and by those outside the community of faith.[15]

The final "anagogical" interpretation has attracted the imagination of many Christians. Much of this interpretation has been viewed through the spectacles provided by biblical passages which, taking their starting point from Psalm 48 and other Jerusalem psalms, came to speak about Jerusalem in ever more extravagant and lyrical language. Sources include texts in Isaiah, Ezekiel, Zechariah, and especially, for Christians, the Apocalypse of John with its glorious vision of a city coming down from heaven. Given the importance of the theme of God's presence in Psalm 48, it is significant to note that the appearance of the "New Jerusalem" in Revelation 21:1–3 is also linked to God's dwelling with humanity:

> Then I saw a new heaven and a new earth; . . . And I saw the holy city, the new Jerusalem, coming down out of heaven from God. . . . And I heard a loud voice from the throne saying,

---

15. Ipgrave and Wilkinson, "Encouraging Reading," 87.

"See, the home of God is among mortals.
He will dwell with them;
they will be his peoples,
and God himself will be with them."

The hope that runs so powerfully throughout Revelation is the culmination of the ideas of the psalmist of Psalm 48, who concluded his song with the instruction: "Tell the next generation that this is God, our God for ever and ever. He will be our guide forever" (Ps. 48:13–14). It is this last form of interpretation, with its focus on hope and the future, which raises sharply a possible source of tension between Jews and Christians in their interpretation of this psalm, and similar biblical texts. The question is this: does the Christian desire or tendency to "spiritualize" what is a very tangible sacredness, linked to a concrete and actual city, mean that something essential is lost in the process of interpretation? Linked to this are two other concerns of a "missional" nature that we also need to address. They affect any conversation between Jews and Christians. The first is whether a Christian "allegorical" interpretation—which draws connections between Jerusalem as the dwelling place of God and the Christian community as the "body of Christ"—can be employed without falling into a supersessionist viewpoint, in which Christianity is considered to have replaced Judaism. Similar concerns are raised by the other "senses" of interpretation of this passage, but they are present most acutely when Christians seek a correlation between the image of the city of Jerusalem and the community of the Christian faith. The second concern is one already raised in this chapter. It relates to the contrast between the "vision" offered by Psalm 48 of a defended fortress and that offered by Psalm 87, which views the city as a goal accessible to all.

There have been many times when the Christian community has seen its vocation as a "defended fortress," but is that what it is really called to be? It is significant that Revelation 21:24 proclaims that "the kings of the earth will bring their glory" into the new Jerusalem. Even the archetypal enemies of God (for that is what this description implies) will find their place in this "holy city." It is telling to read those words alongside the hostility toward the "kings" who, in Psalm 48, eventually flee in fright before God's power displayed in Jerusalem (Ps. 48:4–6). Vital to interreligious conversations are, then, these questions of inclusion and exclusion.

Questions for Reflection

5. What difficulties and opportunities are provided by the different perspectives Jews and Christians bring to the interpretation of a text such as Psalm 48?

6. How appropriate is it for Christians to spiritualize passages such as Psalm 48, which initially referred to concrete physical realities?

7. Thinking about the interpretation that links Jerusalem to the life of the church and to the Christian community, is there a place for the church to be both a "defended fortress" (Psalm 48) and "open and welcoming to all" (Psalm 87)? How does your answer impact your understanding of mission?

Prayer

Jerusalem, "perfection of beauty,"
city cherished and squabbled over,
where hopes have been crucified,
and the colors of resurrection still await the dawn.
We pray for all who love you,
that as well as passion they may learn patience,
that their longings may lead to life,
that their faith in you may bring forth fruit
for the healing of the nations.
Though your stones still cry aloud with the pain of centuries,
drenched with the tears of the one who wept over you,
may the God who called this place his home
give all people wisdom and courage
to discover in you the peace embedded in your name,
so that you may truly become "the joy of all the earth."
Amen.

9

Interreligious Listening, Disagreeing, and Hospitality

Lucinda Mosher and Najah Nadi Ahmad

Do not neglect to show hospitality to strangers, for by doing that some have entertained angels without knowing it.

(Heb. 13:2)

Have you heard the story of Abraham's honored guests? When they came to him and said, "Peace!" he answered, "Peace!" [And he thought to himself, these are] folk unfamiliar to me. Then he went quietly to his family and returned [to those visitors] with a fattened calf. He set it before them, saying, "Will you not eat?"

(Q. 51:25–27, translation ours)

Hospitality. Every essay in this book has been concerned with this concept in some way—often in conversation with notions of mission and welcome. This chapter offers an interreligious response with chapters one through four, seven, and eight particularly in view. It is written by an Anglican theologian who specializes in multifaith concerns and Christian-Muslim comparative theology, in partnership with a Muslim scholar of Islamic law, theology, and spirituality. Together we affirm—as has been made clear in previous chapters—that mission, welcome, and hospitality are at the core of the Christian spiritual and theological tradition. Together, as well, we assert that the same can be said of the Islamic spiritual and theological tradition. For evidence, we turn to the two scriptures: the Bible and the Qur'ān. By "tradition" we mean, in Christianity, the historic Christian creeds, the legacy of the early church fathers, and (for Anglican Christians) the Book of Common Prayer. For Muslims "tradition" means the Sunna (example) of the Prophet Muḥammad, as enshrined in literature known as the *Ḥadīth* (record), as well as the lived and thought theological, juristic, and spiritual practices of Muslim communities throughout the history of the Islamic world. In this chapter, we consider the interplay of interreligious listening and disagreeing, especially as it relates to the imperative to offer hospitality, which Muslims and Christians should take seriously.

Hearing Each Other

In their chapter "Communion as the Discipline of Listening and Talking," Alan Yarborough and Marie Carmel Chery assert that listening "is one of God's qualities"; therefore, we should strive to make it one of ours. Muslims would agree. One of God's Ninety-Nine Beautiful Names is *as-Samī'* (the All-Hearing). If we would be mirrors of God's attributes, it behooves us to listen frequently and generously—and not just to our coreligionists. This was a major lesson of "Christ and People of Other Faiths: The Statement on Interfaith Relations of the Dogmatic & Pastoral Concerns Section Report"—a document created during the 1988 Lambeth Conference.

Lambeth 1988 was the first of these conferences to articulate in depth an Anglican theology of religions, to lay out principles behind and guidelines for interfaith dialogue, to especially speak of a positive place for Islam in an Anglican-Christian worldview, and to give specific attention to warmhearted dialogue with Muslims on theological grounds. The theology of this interfaith argument is profoundly trinitarian and incarnational. Throughout, this document asserts that "the very life of God is a 'being with.'"[1]

---

1. See the Episcopal Church, "Christ and People of Other Faiths (1988)," accessed August 20, 2019, https://www.episcopalchurch.org/library/document/christ-and -people-other-faiths-1988.

Christians may recall that the Christ whom they promise to seek and serve is he who defined the greatest commandment as loving both God *and* neighbor. In the story of the Good Samaritan (Luke 10:30–37), Jesus defined "neighbor" in terms of the *other* who makes a claim on us by virtue of his or her *nearness*.[2] That is, the neighbor is the one who demands that we "be with"; when we are commanded to love God and to love our neighbors *as* ourselves, we are (in effect) commanded to "be with" our neighbors.

When it comes to neighbors whose religions are different from ours, the Lambeth 1988 interfaith documents teach that each encounter is an opportunity to *eavesdrop*: "to overhear what dialogue there may be between God and these people, between the God who calls all into being by a process of sharing and communication, and other peoples in their religious cultures."[3] "Generous Love," a 2008 document from the Anglican Communion Network for Inter Faith Concerns (which was cited in chapter eight by Amos and Sperber), reminds us that "the God who has created our world is generous in grace and rejoices in diversity." Christians know well that "the fruit of the Spirit is love, joy, peace, patience, kindness, generosity, faithfulness, gentleness and self-control" (Gal. 5:22–23). Therefore, "when we meet these qualities in our encounter with people of other faiths, we must engage joyfully with the Spirit's work in their lives and in their communities."[4] We fulfill the command to "be with" our neighbors whose religions are different from ours by taking advantage of opportunities to eavesdrop on our neighbors' own dialogue with the divine, thus opening our soul to our neighbor.

"Listening across difference is difficult," note Yarborough and Chery in chapter two. Yarborough came to realize that "focusing exclusively on

---

2. For the basis of this definition of "neighbor," see Thomas E. Breidenthal, *Christian Households: The Sanctification of Nearness* (Cambridge, MA: Cowley Publication, 1997), 22.

3. See paragraphs 42 and 48 in "Christ and People of Other Faiths (1988)."

4. Anglican Communion Network for Inter Faith Concerns, *Generous Love: The Truth of the Gospel and the Call to Dialogue: An Anglican Theology of Inter Faith Relations* (London: Anglican Consultative Council, 2008), 1–2, https://nifcon .anglicancommunion.org/media/18910/generous_love_a4_with_foreward.pdf.

differences when listening and learning" can prevent one from taking note of commonalities. This is certainly the case in interfaith engagement as well. The differences in worldview, practice, and vocabulary are real. Our disagreements may well be profound. Therefore, improving the *quality* of our disagreeing is time and energy well spent. In chapter three of this volume, the guidance provided by Sarah Hills and Deon Snyman on "disagreeing well"—what it means to do so; how to go about it; where it can lead—has important implications for interfaith understanding. Presuming the goal to be the ability to love people whose beliefs or behaviors seem to oppose ours in every way, learning to "disagree well" is but one step in a complex journey. As they explain, honesty and frankness are essential. Good-quality disagreement, they stress, allows for "plain talking" and makes "space for real emotion to be expressed."[5]

Neither agreeing nor a productive sort of disagreeing can happen unless there is mutual engagement in deep listening and a willingness to acknowledge some common ground—even if that is only a recognition of a shared common humanity. Our increasingly interreligious world provokes a range of responses to the religious Other. Too often, the response takes the form of hostility or competition. A vastly preferable response, as David Lochhead has argued, is an offer of *dialogical relationship*—which, as he defines it, is a relationship of openness and trust that is clear, unambiguous, and has no other purpose than itself. In fact, he asserts (and we concur) that Christians have a biblically based mandate to unconditional openness to their neighbors: an "imperative to seek dialogue and to be open to dialogue whenever and from whomever it is offered."[6] But we note that the Qur'ān also issues Muslims a strongly worded imperative to maintain good relations with one's neighbors: "Worship God; join nothing with Him. Be good to your parents, to relatives, to orphans, to the needy, to neighbors who are near, neighbors who are

---

5. "Generous Love: The Truth of the Gospel and the Call to Dialogue," Anglican Communion, accessed August 15, 2019, https://nifcon.anglicancommunion.org /interactive/_books/default.asp#page0.
6. David Lochhead, *The Dialogical Imperative: A Christian Reflection on Interfaith Encounter* (Maryknoll, NY: Orbis, 1988), 81. In chapter thirteen particularly, Lochhead develops the biblical and theological evidence for this mandate.

strangers" (Q 4:36). This mandate is found as well in numerous prophetic traditions (Sunna), including two *ḥadīth*s narrated in the sound collections of Bukhārī and Muslim.[7] The first states that Prophet Muḥammad has said, "He will not enter Heaven whose neighbor is not secure from his wrongful conduct"; and the second is where he tells us that "Angel Gabriel impressed upon me (the kind treatment) towards the neighbor (so much) that I thought as if he would soon confer upon him the (right) of inheritance." Coupled with this prophetic advice is evidence of Prophet Muḥammad's own practice of trust in and service to his neighbors, most of whom were non-Muslims.

It was in the spirit of openness to dialogue that Rowan Williams, on behalf of the Anglican Communion, was one of twenty-eight international Christian leaders greeted by name when *A Common Word Between Us and You: An Open Letter and Call from Muslim Religious Leaders,* with 138 signatories representing the breadth of Islam, was issued in October 2007 to "Leaders of Christian Churches, everywhere."[8] Much of this epistle is devoted to careful and detailed textual analysis of biblical and Qur'ānic passages—with considerable attention given to the Great Commandment. It asserts that, for Muslims, dialogue is a divine imperative; that exploration of whatever common ground we may share requires that we move beyond mere polite conversation toward an embrace of action in concert with each other; and that striving together for fairness, justice, and mutual goodwill is absolutely necessary for the welfare of the world. Najah recalls that a number of her teachers were among the signatories and that they promoted the message of *A Common Word* among their students of Islamic learning in Egypt. With a growing fondness for this message, Najah believes that a shift of focus from our reliance on dialogue to reliance on knowledge of each other's traditions is essential. This work of hearing the other is closer to the Qur'ānic assertion that we have all been created of different nations "that you may *know* one another" (Q 49.13).

---

7. These are two codified sources for prophetic *ḥadīth*, the soundness of which has been accepted by Muslims as sources of prophetic traditions from the 2nd AH / 9th CE century.
8. *A Common Word*, accessed August 15, 2019, https://www.acommonword.com/.

A Common Word was a carefully crafted call for dialogue. Properly under-stood, *dialogue* (while it is indeed characterized by courtesy and forbearance) is *never* mere polite conversation—a point made in the present volume by Hills and Snyman. Rather, dialogue is dialectical and reciprocal. In other words, unlike debate, its purpose is the gaining of clarity rather than the winning of an argument. *Dialogue* is a technical term for *transformative activity*—a constellation of strategies employed for the purpose of strength-ening relationships or solving problems.[9] That dialogue is by nature transfor-mative was acknowledged by the archbishop of Canterbury and the grand imam of al-Azhar as they agreed (in January 2002) to sustain a formal rela-tionship between their offices: "We believe that friendship which overcomes religious, ethnic and national differences is a gift of the Creator in whom we all believe. . . . We believe that direct dialogue results in restoration of the image of each in the eyes of the other."[10] That is, when we take pains to actu-ally *hear* each other, transformation is much more likely.

In the twenty-first century, when we engage interreligiously, what sort of transformation do we seek? In the arena of interreligious understanding, "witness" and "mission"—closely related terms—are as crucial as they are problematic. As Heaney and Kafwanka did in chapter one, we also assert the importance of mission. But, we ask, what can be meant by *mission*? Must it always be linked to a determination to convert people of some other religion to our own? Heaney and Kafwanka have asserted that "central to partnership in bearing witness to Christ is the importance of a shared common vision of God's holistic love (mission) for the world." We ask, can Christian witness to Christ have a goal other than "conversion"? Can it involve recognition that Muslim, or Hindu, or Jewish neighbors may actually share with Christians a vision of God's love for the world—yet describe God differently from the

---

9. Daniel Yankelovich, *The Magic of Dialogue: Transforming Conflict into Cooperation* (New York: Touchstone, 1999), 12.
10. From the agreement text as published by the Anglican News Service, January 18, 2002, www.anglicannews.org/news/2002/01/archbishop-to-sign-anglican-muslim -agreement.aspx, accessed December 11, 2009.

way in which Christians do? It is indeed important for Christians to examine the relationship between partnership and discipleship. A further question also needs consideration: how do Christians understand partnership when the partner's religion is different from theirs?

In chapter eight, Clare Amos and Daniel Sperber note that "although not entirely negative about the adherents of other religions," several resolutions of the 1897 Lambeth Conference clearly saw Muslims as targets for conversion rather than as interreligious partners. However, over the course of the twentieth century, emphasis on "God's mission" as opposed to "our missions" (as human beings) gained prominence. Such a shift is in evidence in chapter one when Heaney and Kafwanka emphasize that the agent of mission is God. Similarly, in Islamic thought the sovereignty of God is stressed. While the concept of religious calling (*da'wa*) is a concept that has been attached to religious conversion, its most essential feature is the *deliverance* of the message, which is based on the transmission of knowledge. A "theology of presence" now predominates Anglican thinking on interreligious engagement and the transmission of knowledge across differences. According to such "presence theology," when Christians approach adherents of some other religion, they will do so expecting to discover how God has already been speaking to the others and what fresh understandings of God's grace and love they (the Christians) may themselves discover in that encounter.[11]

In their discussion of "Communion as the Discipline of Listening and Talking," Yarborough and Chery note that 1 Peter 2:9 shows us how important it is to remember that we are God's witnesses.[12] Indeed, Christians and Muslims alike are called to bear witness to the truth we believe we have received from God. For Anglican (and many other) Christians, it is summarized in the Nicene Creed; for Muslims, in the *shahada* (the formula affirming God's oneness and Muhammad's prophethood), which is one of the pillars

---

11. For more on a theology of presence, see chapter eight by Amos and Sperber.

12. "But you are a chosen race, a royal priesthood, a holy nation, God's own people, in order that you may proclaim the mighty acts of him who called you out of darkness into his marvelous light."

of their faith. But how are we to bear witness? Muslims take very seriously the Qur'ān's injunctions: "Let there be no compulsion in religion" (Q 2:256) and "We have made you into a just community, so that you may bear witness [to the truth] before others" (Q 2:143). Christians affirm Peter's directive: "Always be ready to make your defense to anyone who demands from you an accounting for the hope that is in you; *yet do it with gentleness and reverence*" (1 Pet. 3:15–16, emphasis added). While expressing it differently, Anglican thought on this matter in recent decades has tended to concur with that of the great Lutheran bishop Krister Stendahl. On more than one occasion, Stendahl said that the task for Christians is to answer the question: "How can I sing my love song to Jesus? How can I sing my song to Jesus with abandon, without disrespecting other religions—without telling negative stories about (or mistreating) others?"[13]

Can there be a candid interreligious conversation about mission and witness? We believe it is possible. We have read carefully the explanation by Heaney and Kafwanka of Anglicanism's five marks of mission. We suggest that three of those marks have particular relevance for those of us who believe that religious diversity—thus interreligious collaboration—is in line with God's will. Muslims, as well as Anglican Christians, are called by scripture and tradition to respond to human need by loving service (mark three); to transform unjust structures of society, to challenge violence of every kind and pursue peace and reconciliation (mark four); and to strive to safeguard the integrity of creation, and sustain and renew the life of the earth (mark five). This calling is very much in line with the "practice norms of interfaith just peacemaking," which include support for nonviolent direct action; use of cooperative conflict resolution; and acknowledgment of responsibility for conflict and injustice coupled with the seeking

---

13. See Krister Stendahl, "Why I Love the Bible: Beyond Distinctions of Intellect and Spirit, an Ever Transforming Affair of the Heart," *Harvard Divinity Bulletin* 35, no. 1 (Winter 2007), https://bulletin.hds.harvard.edu/articles/winter2007/why-i-love-bible.

of repentance and forgiveness.[14] Heaney and Kafwanka urge that "mission formation and discernment . . . take place in the context of intercultural study and intercultural partnership." Their aim is to identify "best practices in such intercultural fellowship." We would say that mission formation must include study of best practices in interreligious fellowship—that we might learn how best to hear each other.

Questions for Reflection

1. Revisit chapter three's guidelines for "disagreeing well." How might they be adapted for use in interfaith situations in your context? Recall your own experience of disagreement (interfaith or otherwise). How did/ might deep listening help you find common ground?

2. In his epistle to the Romans, Paul writes: "Contribute to the needs of the saints; extend hospitality to strangers" (12:13). The author of the epistle to the Hebrews cautions, "Do not neglect to show hospitality to strangers, for thereby some have entertained angels unawares" (13:2). Reflect on occasions when you have extended hospitality to strangers— especially strangers whose religious commitments differed from yours. If you have ever had the sense that you "entertained angels unawares," share something of that experience.

3. In his first epistle, Peter urges: "Always be ready to make your defense to anyone who demands from you an account for the hope that is in you; yet do it with gentleness and reverence" (1 Pet. 3:15–16). Reflect on an occasion in which you were called upon to give "an account of the hope that is in you." If you were able to do so "with gentleness and reverence," how was your accounting received?

4. The Prophet Muḥammad was asked by his companions questions such as: "Where is our Lord?" "When are the best times for us to make supplication?" "When we are praying or making supplication, should

---

14. See Susan Brooks Thistlethwaite, ed., *Interfaith Just Peacemaking: Jewish, Christian, and Muslim Perspectives on the New Paradigm of Peace and War* (New York: Palgrave Macmillan, 2011).

we raise our voice or keep it quiet?" Exegetical literature suggests that, in response to these questions, God reveals the following Qur'ān verse: "When My servants ask you [O Muḥammad] concerning Me, I am indeed close: I listen to the invocation of the supplicant when he calls upon Me. Let them listen to My call, and believe in Me: That they may be led to the right way" (Q. 2:186). Have you yourself ever asked similar questions about praying? Have you been able to listen to God and to sense God listening to you? Reflect on your own attempts to listen to the divine and to other people.

Hearing Scripture

For Anglican-Christian and Sunni-Muslim traditions alike, the recitation (or chanting) of and listening to scripture are important dimensions of worship when gathered in community. Lucinda loves the fact that both the Daily Offices and the Eucharist afford her opportunities to hear scripture read aloud and in abundance. Quotations from scripture comprise integral elements of the liturgy itself—which also directs the faithful to hear at least two or three lengthy Bible passages. The congregation is, in effect, bathed in scripture. Chanting (rather than merely reading aloud) the Psalms is important to many Christians. If one regularly participates in the Daily Offices of Morning and Evening Prayer, one may opt to read one-thirtieth of the Psalter each day, thereby hearing the Psalms in their entirety every month. Indeed, gathered in community, each person who worships according to the Anglican tradition has the opportunity not simply to hear scripture performed for us, but to perform it ourselves for each other and for God.

Just as Anglican-Christians enter into the scriptures deeply through various modes of reception, Muslims too are bathed in the oral/aural beauty of the Qur'ān. Some years ago, Muslim friends came to the bedside of Lucinda's critically ill Christian husband, where they stood and recited the *Fatiḥa* (chapter one of the Qur'ān) and the Throne Verse (Q. 2.255) as part of their supplication for his healing. As Najah confirms, Muslims may well recite or hear the

Fatiḥa (the Opener) at least two dozen times a day. It is an integral element of the five-times-per-day prayer rite and is recited for numerous other reasons. Prophet Muḥammad has reportedly advised Muslims to appoint those with beautiful voices to call for and lead the daily Muslim prayers. Some Muslims maintain the spiritual discipline of preparing for the Friday midday communal prayers (known as *Jum'a*) by meeting on Thursday night for several hours of supplication and poem-singing, punctuated by Qur'ān recitation. Najah herself currently goes to one such circle held in Cambridge, England. During Ramadan—the holiest month of the Islamic calendar—and as part of the prophetic tradition, some Muslims gather at mosques each evening to hear the chanting of one-thirtieth of the Qur'ān. By the end of Ramadan, they have heard the entirety of the Qur'ān recited aloud.

Committing the entire Qur'ān to memory—a discipline undertaken by some Muslims—enables the recitation of any verse or chapter of scripture at a moment's notice. While the Qur'ān may be (and often is) read or recited from memory perfunctorily, there are conventions—called Tajwīd—which those Muslims who wish to accentuate the maximum beauty of their scripture's sound will take pains to learn well. Tajwīd is a science developed by Muslim scholars that studies ways through which Qur'ānic recitation is perfect. These include the tone with which one recites, the rise and fall of the pitch, the placement of accents, the extension of certain syllables—in some instances, enhanced by a melisma (which is to sound what arabesque is to visual art)—in addition to the proper pronunciation of the Arabic letters. Skilled Qur'ān reciters are valued by their community. The great ones are highly respected!

We both have great appreciation for the role the hearing of scripture plays in our respective modes of worship. In each other's respective modes of reading, recitation, and chanting lies something we recognize. But, in addition, we both are veterans of programs that encourage the hearing of scripture interreligiously and studying it dialogically in small, religiously mixed groups. For Najah, this has been through Scriptural Reasoning (SR); for Lucinda, it is the Building Bridges Seminar. SR was an initiative founded by Peter Ochs and David Ford in the 1990s. It has been described as "circles of Jewish,

Christian, and Muslim text scholars and theologians who bring both their sciences and their faiths to the table while they engage together in extended periods of [comparative] scriptural study."[15] Religiously neutral meeting places are preferred, as they are perceived as being equally hospitable to all participants. A given SR circle may choose to meet weekly or monthly or as often as the group wishes. During a typical meeting, selected biblical and Qur'ānic passages are read aloud, then discussed.

While working on her doctoral thesis at Oxford, Najah spent three years participating in—and later coorganizing—the monthly SR meetings at the Oxford Centre for Muslim-Christian Studies. The meetings took place at the heart of the historic Oxford University and attracted academics, church, and mosque leaders, as well as general believers from both faiths. She and her Christian coorganizer prepared and circulated chosen passages from both scriptures on a single topic before the meeting. Both were surprised at how easy it was to find passages from the Qur'ān and the Bible tackling the same theological, historical, social, and spiritual topics they wished to address. On the day of the SR gathering, Najah would recite the Qur'ānic passages herself, using her Tajwīd training, or would ask for a volunteer from the attendees. SR discussions around selected Bible and Qur'ān passages have opened doors of understanding, rather than plain agreement, between all attendees. At times, Najah recalls, it was challenging to assure all participants that the SR meeting was a safe and honest space for expressing thoughts on scriptures. When this basic idea is established among all, openings of soul and intellect follow.

The Building Bridges Seminar, for which Lucinda is the assistant academic director, is often compared to SR. It has, however, a different methodology. Founded in 2002 by George Carey (then archbishop of Canterbury), this Christian-Muslim dialogue was sustained from 2003 through 2012 by his successor, Rowan Williams. While it is now under the stewardship of Georgetown University, Anglicans remain very much involved. Different from SR, the Building Bridges Seminar comprises a single annual gathering

---

15. The Journal of Scriptural Reasoning Forum, "What Is SR?" accessed January 27, 2013, http://jsrforum.lib.virginia.edu/writings/OchFeat.html.

by invitation only—and is very definitely a dialogue of experts. Some fifteen Muslims and fifteen Christians spend four days together in close reading of texts, which includes long sessions in predesignated groups of seven or eight participants. Passages from the Bible and the Qur'ān, but sometimes from various premodern and modern sources as well, are chosen for their usefulness in exploring that year's theme. Although it is expected that these texts will have been read in advance, they are introduced by means of exegetical lectures during plenary sessions. The seminar has explored revelation, justice, sin, community, and many more complex and multifaceted topics. A small group session typically features some time to review the day's assigned texts. Participants then take turns pointing out passages—or even single words—about which they have questions or comments that they would like the group to discuss. Having created an agenda, a passage is read aloud and discussion ensues. The proceedings of each annual convening are edited and published, thus providing resources for others to use in dialogical or classroom settings.

While their methodologies do differ substantially, what both Scriptural Reasoning and the Building Bridges Seminar demonstrate is the possibility and value of interreligious hearing and discussion of scripture. Not only are both projects models for interreligious learning, both are models for fruitful interreligious disagreement. In fact, Rowan Williams has often cited one of the purposes of the Building Bridges Seminar to be "improving the quality of our disagreements." The same can be said of SR.

Questions for Reflection

5. How would you explain to an adherent of another religion when, where, how, and with whom you read scripture?

6. What is your own experience of reading aloud, chanting, and reciting scripture? Do you have a preference?

7. Have you had the opportunity to hear a recitation of someone else's scripture? If so, what can you remember and share about that experience?

8. If you were to engage in a scripture-based interreligious dialogue, what three passages of scripture would you most like to bring to the table for discussion? What two or three themes? Explain your choices.

Hearing the Spirit

In "The Truth Shall Make You Free" (Lambeth Conference, 1988), we find the assertion (in paragraph 48) that Christian encounter with people of other faiths is an opportunity "to overhear what dialogue there may be between God and these people—between the God who calls all into being by a process of sharing and communication, and other peoples in their religious cultures."[16] The document implies here that the Spirit of God not only blows wherever it chooses, but the hearing of it extends beyond the bounds of the Christian community.

How might the Spirit make itself heard? In some understandings, angels are spirits or agents of God. This brings us to the scripture passages we placed at the head of this chapter. "Do not neglect to show hospitality to strangers," says the author of the epistle to the Hebrews, "for by doing that some have entertained angels without knowing it" (Heb. 13:2). Jews, Christians, and Muslims alike point to Abraham as one who had such an experience. "Have you heard the story of Abraham's honored guests?" God asks in the Qur'ān (Q. 51:25–27). Muslims often point to this passage of the Qur'ān as their warrant for offering hospitality to strangers. They might also recall a *ḥadīth* in which the Prophet says to someone in his community, "O Abu Dharr, if you cook broth, add extra water to it and give some to your neighbor." Therefore, it is now a custom in many Muslim cultures for people to share some of whatever they have cooked with their neighbor. "I used to see this happen since I was a little girl visiting my grandmother in the summers in Istanbul," a Muslim colleague said recently. Relatedly, according to Islamic tradition, Noah's Ark came to rest on dry land on the tenth day of Muharram—the first month of the Islamic year. Some Muslims commemorate this by making "Noah's pudding," then distributing it to their neighbors. Our Turkish Muslim friends in the US and UK tell us they are taught to define "neighbor"

---

16. The Lambeth Conference, "The Truth Shall Make You Free," Anglican Communion, 1988, accessed October 29, 2019, https://nifcon.anglicancommunion.org/media/129597/lam88_section_report.pdf.

as "anyone living within forty blocks of our home." Imagine the implications of this definition in places like New York City or London, which feature block after block of tall apartment buildings!

In chapter four, Gloria Mapangdol and Paulo Ueti explain that a literal translation of 1 Peter 4:9 would read "Pursue hospitality." The original Greek implies continuous action. It is a reference to the practice of generosity and courtesy shown to those who find themselves far from home. It describes a ritual of reciprocity between guest and host expressed in both material and spiritual benefits. Such reciprocity can indeed be developed and enjoyed— even between people of many different religions. Both the Bible and the Islamic tradition assert that the best preparation for the hereafter has less to do with prayer and praise and more to do with offering hospitality. Jesus exhorts his followers to care for the hungry, the thirsty, the stranger, those in need of clothing, the sick, and the imprisoned (Matt. 25:31–46). The *Ḥadīth* reports that the Prophet Muḥammad once said that "anyone who believes in God and the Last Day should entertain his guest generously."[17] The Qur'ān, in chapter 107, says: "Have you seen the one who denies religion? That is the one who drives away the orphan and does not urge feeding the indigent. So, woe to those who pray formally but are heedless of what they are praying, those who strive [for their piety] to be seen, yet refuse [to offer] small kindnesses."[18] In such passages—as also in Heb. 13:2 and Q. 51:25–27—priority is given to making visitors comfortable and meeting their bodily needs. Any witnessing to the truth we have perceived, or to the hope dwelling within us, will take place by means of our acts of kindness and not by means of proselytizing.

Mapangdol and Ueti include an interesting section, the header for which speaks of "loyalty to Jesus." We would remind our Christian readers that Muslims are also "loyal to Jesus," the story of whose birth figures prominently in the Qur'ān. Islamic literature portrays Jesus primarily as an

---

17. *Sahih Al-Bukhari*, vol. 8:73, 47.
18. Seyyed Hossein Nasr et al., eds., *The Study Quran: A New Translation and Commentary* (New York: HarperOne, 2015), 1566; adapted slightly.

ascetic teacher whose teachings include lessons on hospitality. According to one report, "Jesus said to his disciples. . . . 'As for the Lord, you must love Him with all your heart. Then you must love your neighbor as yourself.'"[19] In Islamic collections of reports about Jesus, he is often addressed by inquirers as "Messenger of God," "Word of God," and "Spirit of God" (see Q. 4:171).[20] For example, one such report says: "Jesus prepared food for his disciples. When they had eaten, he himself washed their hands and feet. They said to him, 'Spirit of God, it is we, rather, that should do this.' He replied, 'I have done this so that you would do it to those whom you teach.'"[21] Again, each religious community has its particular understanding of what is meant by "the Spirit of God." Can we trust that each does indeed hear in its own way what that Spirit is saying? Interestingly, the major Qur'ānic chapter that details the story of Jesus is named after his mother. Mary, a spiritual and sacred figure in the Islamic tradition and Muslim communities, is extolled for her exemplary wisdom and piety.

Mapandgol and Ueti talk about how, on the road to Emmaus, the risen Jesus first made himself a stranger then made himself a neighbor. This story, they say, models the appropriateness of establishing contact, talking to, and connecting with others. According to Luke 24:17, they say, "Jesus is interested in engaging with these people and their lives." On the road to Emmaus, they note, Jesus matches the pace of the people he encounters, rather than expecting them to match his. If we would be like Jesus, it behooves us to try this conversational technique with our other-faith neighbors: we can be interested in the details of their lives, adjusting our pace to theirs, offering hospitality whenever we can.

---

19. Abu Hayyan al-Tawhidi, *Risala fi al-Sadaqa wa al-Sadiq.* Included in Tarif Khalidi, ed. and trans., *The Muslim Jesus: Sayings and Stories in Islamic Literature* (Cambridge, MA: Harvard University Press, 2001), 147.
20. For numerous examples, see Khalidi, *Muslim Jesus.*
21. Abu al-Husayn Warram ibn Abi Firas, *Majmu'a,* 1:83. Included in Khalidi, *Muslim Jesus,* 199.

Prayer

Gracious, Compassionate God,

we thank you for humanity's glorious diversity.

We offer thanks, in particular, for neighbors, acquaintances, friends, and family members who strive toward truth and beauty, motivated by religious commitments different from our own.

We are grateful that in their faithfulness to their own path and their questions about ours, they encourage us to give a clear account of where we stand—what we believe, and why; how we worship and why.

We are grateful for the ways they inspire us to explore afresh the depth and breadth of our own tradition.

We are grateful for the many ways they encourage us to recall the generosity of your love.

You have provided us with exemplars of hospitality.

May we be open to opportunities to welcome strangers as honored guests—ready to greet them with a sign of peace, ready to do so in your name, O Merciful One.

Amen/Amin.

10

Interreligious Sharing, Mutuality, and Partnership

Samy Fawzy Shehata and Nayla Tabbara

Whoever does not love does not know God, for God is love . . . Those who abide in love aabide in God, and God abides in them.

(1 John 4:8, 16)

Word of the Prophet: By He who has my life in His hands, you will not enter Paradise if you do not believe, and you will not believe until you love each other. Shall I tell you how to love each other? By spreading peace amongst you.

(Ṣaḥīḥ Muslim 54)

Reading chapters five through eight brings to the fore themes of generosity (chapter five) and mutuality (chapter six) amidst ecumenical (chapter seven) and interreligious (chapter eight) diversity. Sharing in ways that benefit one another and looking for opportunities for Christians and Muslims to partner for the common good are themes that we hold as sacred in our contexts in Egypt and Lebanon. Our task is to review these chapters, discerning where we see themes and practices that resource interreligious partnership and discerning where further opportunities might arise.

Bishop Samy Fawzy Shehata is an Anglican area bishop of North Africa within the Diocese of Egypt and North Africa and the Horn of Africa. The diocese, within the province of Jerusalem and the Middle East, is one of the most diverse in the world. It extends over eight countries, including Algeria, Tunisia, Libya, Egypt, Ethiopia, Eritrea, Somalia, and Djibouti. With over one hundred congregations, the vision of the diocese is to reach the unreached, grow disciples, serve its neighbors, work for unity among Christians, and deepen relationships with all.

Nayla Tabbara is a Lebanese Muslim woman theologian and university professor in religious studies. In 2006, with Christian and Muslim friends, she founded Adyan, an organization to promote diversity, solidarity, and human dignity. She currently directs the Institute of Citizenship and Diversity Management at Adyan. This is the academic branch of the foundation. Adyan's other branches are its advocacy and policy dialogue branch (the Rashad Center for Cultural Governance), its civic engagement branch, and its media branch that includes the *Taadudiya* (pluralism) platform, which reaches 30 million people each year promoting a positive narrative on pluralism and advocating against sectarianism and extremism.

Hearing Each Other

Chapter five laid out a vision for "disciplined sharing." Janice Price and John Kapya Kaoma emphasized the grassroots nature of sharing and identified the importance of these relationships set within the wider context of structures. Particularly, they held up the Jerusalem collection (2 Cor. 8–9; Gal. 2:10) as structured or institutional generosity. The church of Jerusalem was suffering from severe food shortages. Because of interaction between church leaders, support was sent from Macedonia to Jerusalem to alleviate their suffering. Price and Kaoma are right to note that this is "disciplined" generosity because it is discerned and administered through existing lines of leadership and fellowship. However, more can be said. This is "disciplined" generosity because it is an expression of the believers' discipleship and it is a deepening of their discipleship. Paul writes that the administration of the gift not only meets the needs of the people but is a thanksgiving to God (2

Cor. 9:12). In Islam also, alongside *zakat* (legal almsgiving), one of the five pillars of practice, generosity is the mark of the believers and a criteria of righteousness (*Al Baqara* 2:177).

In chapter six, Cornelia Eaton and James Stambaugh provided us with an image of mutuality where God is the great weaver knitting us together. From two distinct cultural locations, they sought to weave together an understanding and vision of mutuality. From a Christian perspective, mutuality means relationship with Jesus Christ and other believers. It is what it means to be an intentional disciple. Eaton and Stambaugh largely shy away from the content of the faith in mutuality to focus on mutuality in practice. Thus, they depict mutuality as looking to the interests of others, prayer, hospitality, storytelling, listening, and partnership. This mutuality and interconnectedness is the "beauty way" (*hozhó*). Even amidst brokenness, the fundamental reality is that we are all children of God. The "beauty way" is a recognition of this and a call to deeper community in acts of restoration. The authors also ask if mutuality is possible in situations of injustice. This, we would submit, is where the concept of solidarity becomes important. Solidarity is one of the most important concepts in Islam. In early Muslim history it was solidarity that helped the community to survive after they were thrown out of their homes. Solidarity was seen between rich and poor and between the host community and these first Muslim refugees.

No doubt Eaton and Stambaugh paint a compelling picture of a central element of mutuality. An appeal, however, to the person of Christ is an appeal to a theological commitment. Christians claim they act in certain ways in the world because they believe certain things about God in Christ. This raises a question not only about mutuality in right action but also mutuality in right beliefs. While Eaton and Stambaugh argue that Christians in mutuality do not need to be in full agreement, questions remain. Given a diversity of theological understandings, how do we know we are practicing mutuality? When might divergences in belief (with the implications this has for practice) threaten mutuality? In interreligious settings the questions become more acute. How can we have mutuality and solidarity when it appears that religious identity and commitment are what created the divides in the first place?

There is no substitute for generous dialogue and the cultivating of inter-religious friendship. Thankfully, history provides us with testimony to the transformative power of such interreligious encounter. In apartheid South Africa people from different faiths and life philosophies worked together for social justice. This is clearly visible in the life and work of South African Muslim liberation theologian Farid Esack. For Esack, interreligious mutuality was lived. It meant having the same mind, the same objective and intention, and the same values, beyond the differences of faith and religious practice. Such mutuality is possible between people from different backgrounds and in situations of human rights abuse when people work together to redress situations of injustice and oppression. In other words, mutuality cannot be a retreat from reality.

When human rights are being violated, religionists must avoid fabricating some sort of weak harmony in interreligious dialogue meetings. Such "harmony" might, in the end, deafen and blind us to the suffering of others. This is not interreligious mutuality. It is escape from reality. Both the Bible and the Qur'ān condemn such false comfort. Interreligious mutuality means we work for each other's good toward liberation and transformation for all. The Qur'ān says to all believers: "O you who believe, be upholders of justice—witnesses for Allah, even though against (the interest of) yourselves or the parents, and the kinsmen" (*An Nisa'* 4:135). It also says, concerning diversity: "For each of you We have made a law and a method. Had Allah willed, He would have made a single community of people, but (He did not), so that He may test you in what He has given to you. Strive, then, to excel each other in good deeds. To Allah is the return for all of you. Then Allah shall tell you about that in which you disputed" (*Al Ma'ida* 5:48). The invitation is clear. Mutuality is lived when we strive for the common good and believe that diversity is willed by God. It is lived when we do not stop at theological disputations but, trusting in God, use our energy and time responsibly on this earth for the sake of a better world.

What Eaton and Stambaugh avoid in chapter six, Anne Burghardt and John Gibaut directly address in chapter seven. Ecumenical dialogues are theological. Among Christians, they seek commonality not only in action toward one another, vital though that is, but in shared faith commitments. Burghardt and Gibaut note it is particularly the biblical vision of communion (*koinonia*) that has allowed for renewed agreement as well as cooperation. The vision of such communion begins with a vision of who God is and what God calls his people to be and do. The church is called to live for God, for others, and for creation.

In more recent years, this call of God to mission has been defined as testifying to the faith alongside advocacy for those who are marginalized and service to all people regardless of their faith commitments. Beyond ecumenical settings, we are left asking, what does a Christian understanding of God's calling mean for life and service amidst people of other faiths and with people of other faiths? Further, given the recent emergence of "receptive ecumenism," how might our vision of God and practice of faith change across religious differences? What might Christians receive afresh from people of other faiths to guide them in their discipleship and witness? As a Christian and a Muslim, we are particularly drawn to the theme of friendship as a lived reality and an important theological commitment in both our traditions.

In its dialogue with other religions, the Qur'ān, especially with the "People of the Book," calls for meeting one another and it calls for dialogue: "O mankind! We have indeed created you from a male and a female, and made you nations and tribes that you may come to know one another" (*Al Hujurat* 49:13). To know one another does not mean setting aside our religious beliefs and theological differences. For a genuine meeting to take place, we must come together as our true selves. This means an acceptance of diversity and a heart open to learn. We need to recognize the authenticity of the spiritual experience of the other even if we do not recognize their dogma or belief system. When such a spirit is present, friendship becomes possible.

An example of interreligious friendship is found in the nineteenth-century story of the Emir Abdel Kader and Charles Eynard. Abdel Kader was a Muslim hero and leading Sufi scholar, and Eynard was a Swiss Protestant. Recognizing each other's spiritual path, they developed a friendship "in God." Abdel Kader called Eynard "the well-beloved who we have loved before the face of God Most High," the "one who knows God" (*'arif billah*), and the "well-beloved in God."[1] Such acclaim calls to mind a *ḥadīth* (tradition of the prophet):

> The prophet has said: "Among the worshippers of God, there are people who are neither prophets nor martyrs, but whom the prophets and martyrs will envy at the Last Day." One asked him: "who are they?" He replied: "these are people who love each other by the spirit of God among them, without having links of parenthood, nor goods in common. By God! their faces are alight, and they are guided by the light, they will not have fear when people are in fear nor will they be afflicted when people will be afflicted [at the day of judgment]" and he quoted the Qur'an: "In truth, the well-beloved of God are sheltered from all fear, and they will never be afflicted." (*Yunus* 10: 62)

It is interesting to note that this *ḥadīth* is not speaking specifically about Muslims. It refers to worshipers in general.

In chapter eight, Amos and Sperber provide a Christian and Jewish reading of a meeting place sacred to Jews, Christians, and Muslims. Like a city, interreligious dialogue and mutual understanding can be untidy and labyrinthine. Yet it is in the proximity of one with another in the busy streets of our lives that misconceptions and misunderstandings can be corrected and deeper understanding forged. Amos and Sperber do not avoid the untidiness of interreligious understanding but rather provide two readings of the holiness and nature of Zion. God is present in Jerusalem and protects Jerusalem both in warding off those who would threaten her and in welcoming those who need a home (Ps. 48, 87). Such themes might complement one another or they might be set against one another. Are we required to choose between

---

1. Ahmed Bouyerdene, *Emir Abd el-Kader: Hero and Saint of Islam,* trans. Gustavo Polit (Bloomington, IN: World Wisdom, 2012), 187–92.

a God who defends us against those who are different and a God who invites all to God's blessing? These are questions that Muslims and Christians, as well as Jews and Christians and Muslims and Jews, need to ask each other.

It is true that our religious traditions hold places that are sacred. They are sacred, surely, because they are places that open up access to the divine. Yet it is clear from all our traditions that in the hierarchy of sacredness—humans come first. The Qur'ān depicts an event that happened before humans were sent to earth. God asks the angels to prostrate in front of Adam (*'an Al Kahf* 18:50). Another verse in the Qur'ān, reminding us of what was set down in the Jewish law, says: "Because of that, We decreed for the Children of Israel that whoever slays a soul for other than a soul, or for corruption in the land, it shall be as if he had slain mankind altogether; and whoever saves the life of one, it shall be as if he had saved the life of all mankind. Our messengers have already come to them with clear proofs, but after that many of them still commit excesses in the land" (*Al Ma'ida* 5:32). The sacredness of human life is a shared commitment across our traditions. In the Muslim legal tradition, the law (*shari'a*) has a fivefold finality (*maqasid ash-shari'a*), the first among them being the preservation of human life. Human life is sacred, for God's spirit dwells within us: "I have proportioned him and breathed of My Spirit in him" (*Al Hijr*, 15:49; see also Gen. 2:7; Ps. 51:10–11; Job 27:3; 1 Cor. 6:19–20). In the Bible, humans are made in the very image of God (Gen. 1:26; 5:1; 2 Cor. 3:18; James 3:9).[2] Despite these strong traditions of human sanctity we have too often prioritized—sometimes for sociopolitical reasons, historical reasons, and/or economic reasons—territory over people.

---

2. See Matthias Morgenstern, "The Deconstruction of the *Adam and Eve* Narrative in Bereshit Rabbah: Variations on the Significance of the Name 'Adam,' the *Image of God* and the Fall and Redemption of Man(kind) in Jewish Late Antiquity," in *New Approaches to Human Dignity in the Context of Qur'ānic Anthropology: The Quest for Humanity*, ed. Rüdiger Braun and Hüseyin I. Çiçek (Newcastle upon Tyne: Cambridge Scholars, 2017), 50–54; and Richard S. Park, *Constructing Civility: The Human Good in Christian and Islamic Political Theologies* (Notre Dame: University of Notre Dame Press, 2017), 105–29.

Questions for Reflection

1. What are the strengths and weaknesses of generosity that is organized by an institution? What are the strengths and weaknesses of giving to those in need as an individual (see chapter five)?
2. How important to you is common belief for common belonging (see chapter six)?
3. In contexts of oppression or injustice, what type of interreligious encounters should be encouraged?
4. What forms of solidarity can be expressed with people from other religions/beliefs?

Hearing Scripture

The themes of friendship, the peace of the community, and generosity that we consider central to chapters five through eight are central to our faith commitment as a Christian and as a Muslim. This is borne out in text after text in both the Bible and the Qur'ān.

The Qur'ān presents generosity as the mark of believers and of righteousness:

> Righteousness is not that you turn your faces to the East and the West; but righteousness is that one believes in Allah and the Last Day and the angels and the Book and the Prophets, and gives wealth, despite his/her love for it, to relatives, and to orphans, the helpless, the wayfarer, and to those who ask, and (spends) in (freeing) slaves and observes the Salāh (prayers) and pays Zakat-and (the act of) those who fulfill their covenant when they enter into a covenant, and, of course, those who are patient in hardship and suffering when in battle! Those are the ones who are truthful, and those are the God-fearing. (*Al Baqara* 2:177)[3]

---

3. Qur'ānic English translations are inspired by the Royal Aal al-Bayt Institute translation at www.altafsir.com

Because of this, *zakat* is not only considered financial almsgiving, but every act of giving from what one has is considered *zakat*. For a person endowed with knowledge, sharing this knowledge generously, without asking for renumeration, is performing *zakat*. Similarly, *Sadaqa* (generous giving besides the legal *zakat*) is not only financial but extends to all acts for the common good. A tradition from the Prophet Muḥammad says: "Charity (*sadaqa*) is due upon every joint of the people for every day upon which the sun rises. Being just between two people is charity. Helping a man with his animal and lifting his luggage upon it is charity. A kind word is charity. Every step that you take towards the mosque is charity, and removing harmful things from the road is charity" (*Bukhari*, 2827).[4]

Adyan, from its foundation, has worked for the common good and advocated for rights not by putting faith commitments aside but by recognizing the contributions of different religious and philosophical belongings. This recognition is not synonymous with sectarianism. Adyan is convinced that faith does not confine human beings to a specific sectarian sphere. Rather, it should elevate them toward fraternity, empathy, and solidarity with others in order to work together for the common good and to build peace on the foundations of partnership, interaction, reconciliation, and the sharing of spiritual goods. Members of Adyan are mindful of celebrating the other as the voice of God or the voice of the indescribable in our lives. Adyan, thus, is a foundation for pluralism, solidarity, and human dignity that works for inclusive citizenship, community resilience, freedom of religion or belief, and spiritual solidarity. According to Adyan, people who abide by spiritual solidarity in their life are those who carry within them all other communities, to the extent that they uphold others' rights and carry their fears and hopes with empathy. Those who are imbued with this spirit strive for peace, reconciliation, equality, and social justice, and have at heart the dignity of each human being and the rights of all.

---

4. Translation taken from https://abuaminaelias.com/forty-hadith-nawawi/.

Arguably, for Christians, it is the biblical vision of communion (*koinonia*) that brings together the themes of peace, generosity, and friendship. It is because of the generosity or grace of God, in Christ, that Christians know peace and know friendship with one another (Phil. 3:4–16; 1 Cor. 10:16–17; 2 Cor. 8:9; 1 John 1:1–3). While *koinonia* cannot be reduced to these things, the offer and benefits of friendship are an important and ancient way for Christians to think about fellowship with God (Isa. 41:8; James 2:23) and each other (Prov. 18:24; John 15:13–15). The concept of the church as communion (*koinonia*) harmonizes several scriptural images particularly related to the church as the body of Christ (1 Cor. 12:12–31) and the people of God (Acts 2:42–45). These images point to the notion that the church is a supernatural organism birthed and brought to life by the Holy Spirit. The church is a fellowship sustained by the outpouring of divine grace. This closeness, or friendship, of the Spirit with and in the church opens up space for ecumenical friendship. For it puts the stress not on institutional arrangements but on the gracious gifts of God. A stress on the church as the body of Christ and the people of God in communion with God brings Protestants, Catholics, and the Orthodox together in Egypt.

In seeking friendship among Christians, Egyptian Anglicans see their church as a "bridge church." This means friendship is about connecting people. Such connection is lived out in three different directions. Locally, Anglicans live together as Egyptians and seek the best for their country. The specific nature of such local service will be considered below when the peace of the community will be the focus. Suffice it to say, friendship involves space to meet and space to imagine life-giving ways of renewing community. Nationally, Anglicans play their part in the Egypt Council of Churches, aiming to unite the churches in Egypt in shared meetings and projects. The mission of the Anglican Church in Egypt as a "bridge church" is evident in the mutual friendships with Coptic, Catholic, and Protestant churches. Globally, the diocese participates in and takes seriously the dialogue between Anglicans and Oriental Orthodox churches. Mutual agreements were signed on the nature of Christ and on the procession of the Holy Spirit that teach the

church not only about the nature of friendship between humans but friendship (or *koinonia*) with God.[5]

The biblical understanding of the church as communion opens the door
for work and ministry with all humanity. There is a degree of communion
between Christians and Muslims in Egypt based on belief in God, common
moral values, and the one destiny. In the Egyptian context, Christians and
Muslims have been shaped by 1,400 years of common heritage of faith. That
Anglicans claim friendship, and even communion, with God carries with it
the responsibility to be friends with all Egyptians. Because this call to friendship is biblical, theological dialogue becomes important.

Doctrinal dialogue in Egypt includes meetings and explorations in which
doctrinal and philosophical issues are discussed. Muslims and Christians discuss and learn from one another about faith commitments in this context of
religious pluralism. Doctrinal dialogue is closely linked to formal dialogue,
but it is formal dialogue that takes on a more scholarly form. For example,
there has been hopeful and constructive exchange between theologians from
Al Azhar University and Cambridge University in the UK. In 2006, the grand
mufti, along with the bishop of Egypt, addressed the faculty of divinity at
Cambridge to celebrate an exchange program between Al Azhar University
and Cambridge.[6] In that lecture, Sheikh Ali Gomaa noted the importance
of "clear, sober and scholarly" approaches to the Qur'ān. From such study
Muslims and Christians learn that God has "forbidden the killing of inno-
cents" and that God willed diversity so that human knowledge would be

---

5. Anglican-Oriental International Commission, *Christology: Agreed Statement*
(Cairo, 2014), https://www.anglicancommunion.org/media/103502/Anglican-Oriental
-Orthodox-Agreed-Statement-on-Christology-Cairo-2014.pdf;   Anglican-Oriental
Orthodox International Commission, *The Procession and Work of the Holy Spirit: Agreed
Statement* (Dublin, 2017), https://www.anglicancommunion.org/media/312561/the
-procession-and-work-of-the-holy-spirit-dublin-agreed-statement.pdf.
6. "Grand Mufti to Speak at Cambridge," University of Cambridge, November 2,
2006, https://www.cam.ac.uk/news/grand-mufti-to-speak-at-cambridge.

richer and deeper (*Al Hujurat* 49:13). For the grand mufti, there "is no more powerful a weapon against extremism than correct education."[7]

The grand mufti and the bishop demonstrated the importance of scholarship in interreligious work for peace that also always proceeds from friendship and moves toward deeper friendship. The publication of books and statements that clarify theological misconceptions are all the richer for such personal journeys, encounters, and the growth of friendships. Key doctrinal dialogues give confidence to believers that indeed Christians and Muslims worship the same God. We worship the one God. We worship the God who is one and sovereign, the God of mercy involved in the world.[8] Such a spirit is part of an Anglican approach to dialogue. In 1998, the Lambeth Conference affirmed the doctrinal or theological nature of interfaith dialogue as a "common and mutual exploration of the ultimate significance of the human condition." This does not mean that Christians abandon the Gospel or that dialogue demands we ignore the deep differences in the two great faiths (especially in relation to the nature of God and Jesus Christ). On the contrary, "open and honest discussion" for Anglicans includes testifying to the grace of God found in the Prince of Peace.[9]

Questions for Reflection

5. What text from another tradition—for example, from the Hebrew Bible (Old Testament) or Qur'ān—has resonated with you? Why?

6. What unrealized opportunities or dangers do you see in such interreligious reading of texts?

7. How would you help believers from different traditions reflect on the sacredness of human life in relation to the sacredness of land?

---

7. Sheikh Ali Gomaa, "Building Bridges of Understanding," *Cambridge Interfaith Programme,* November 17, 2006, https://www.interfaith.cam.ac.uk/resources/lecturespapersandspeeches/buildingbridgesofunderstanding.

8. Michael Ipgrave, "One, Living, Reasonable: The God of Christianity and Islam," *Journal of Shi'a Islamic Studies* 1, no. 3 (2008): 19–32.

9. Cited in Douglas Pratt, "From Edinburgh to Georgetown: Anglican Interfaith Bridge-Building," *Anglican Theological Review* 96, no. 1 (2014): 24.

Hearing the Spirit

We are led by the Spirit of God to glorify God in our lives. For Shehata, this means that Anglicans in Egypt seek to be generous, seek to be friends to all, and work for the peace and welfare of the community. Such witness is led by the Spirit and amidst such witness the Spirit is experienced and heard. For Tabbara, it means recognizing the Spirit of God in other world religions, and the actions of God in interpersonal relations based on empathy and solidarity. Her work with Adyan also shapes an understanding and practice of friendship, generosity, and peace through valuing diversity, promoting solidarity, and defending human dignity.

Following ten years of working for triannual strategic plans and constantly evaluating, monitoring, and upgrading them, Adyan took the occasion of its tenth anniversary (2016) to assess its achievements and to discern targets for the next ten years. Four main goals were set for 2026. First, in the Lebanese context, Adyan will contribute to moving Lebanon away from sectarianism and toward becoming an inclusive, diverse, and democratic state. Second, at the Levant level and with a specific focus on Iraq and Syria, Adyan will help resource the capacities needed for new leadership that will usher in a multicultural renaissance for the Levantine countries. Third, at the Arab regional level, Adyan will help foster an acceptance of cultural, political, and religious pluralism as a sociopolitical good. Fourth, at the global level, Adyan will aid in the development of policies that create resilience against all forms of extremism and nurture cohesive and stable societies.[10] These goals grow out of Adyan's fourfold set of values of cultural and religious diversity, human dignity and individual specificity (that is to say, people can never be reduced to their religious identity at the expense of human individuality), partnership and spiritual solidarity, and peace and social justice.

Friendship

Following September 11, 2001, a historic document was signed by the Grand Imam of al-Azhar al-Sharif, Dr. Mohamed Sayed Tantawy, and the

---

10. For more information, see http://adyanfoundation.org/.

archbishop of Canterbury, George Carey.[11] This document set out hopes and practicalities for ongoing exploration and exchange between Christians and Muslims. This dialogue between the Anglican Communion and al-Azhar al-Sharif began with an affirmation of friendship as a "gift from the Creator." Such friendship "overcomes religious, ethnic and national differences."[12] Such friendship develops through formalized dialogues but it also develops through day-to-day exchanges, family ties, and community belongings. By building on such expressions of friendship, more intentional witness and ministry in what might be called *life dialogue* emerges.

Life dialogue concentrates on projects of common concern. This type of dialogue is often designed to encourage common action. Based at St. Mark's Pro-Cathedral in downtown Alexandria, the Arkan Center is a place where Egyptian youth from all corners of society, both Christian and Muslim, come together and create art. The Arkan Center supports talented young artists by providing facilities for producing and displaying youth artwork, and cultural and artistic workshops. In the Arkan Center, artistic expression opens up forums for discussion that invite people to new perspectives and ideas. It is a quiet challenge to intolerant attitudes. As the lives of youth from many different backgrounds intersect, bridges of peace and friendship are built, gradually replacing walls of intolerance and fear.

Gusour Cultural Center at All Saints' Cathedral in Cairo seeks to provide opportunities for all society members of all cultural backgrounds to build bridges of understanding, acceptance, and cooperation through art, music, educational, and cultural activities. One of the goals of Gusour is to help the deaf and the hearing-impaired integrate with the wider society by organizing Egyptian sign-language courses that enable the trainees to communicate with

---

11. "Archbishop to Sign Anglican-Muslim Agreement," Anglican Communion News Service, January 18, 2002, https://www.anglicannews.org/news/2002/01/archbishop-to-sign-anglican-muslim-agreement.aspx.
12. Anglican Communion, "An Agreement for Dialogue between the Anglican Communion and al-Azhar al-Sharif," February 2, 2002, https://www.anglicancommunion.org/media/111577/An-agreement-for-dialogue-between-the-Anglican-Communion-and-al-Azhar-al-Sharif.pdf.

the deaf community in their own language. These courses also cover types of deafness, problems deaf people face, and their relationship to hearing communities. Bringing people together in friendship and for friendship changes the world. It reminds us that theological commitments and a commitment to peace are never abstract. Peace is a practice. Working for "the peace of the city" means dialogue.

Adyan is based on friendship between Christians and Muslims. It was founded by four Christian and Muslim friends and one friend who does not define herself by her religious belonging. Through its networks, Adyan seeks to establish and nurture interreligious friendships. Its youth network consists of around three hundred young people from all over Lebanon. Together they have learned about each other and provided valuable public service to their communities. A similar network of religious leaders, Christian and Muslim men and women, was launched in 2019 as a forum of religious actors for religious social responsibility. Other networks that serve reconciliation and social cohesion include a families network that gathers Christian, Muslim, and mixed couples together to share the values they live by and to work on strengthening friendship and community in their respective contexts. An ambassador's network of young men and women from Christian and Muslim and nonreligious backgrounds in Lebanon, and from Christian, Muslim, Yezidi, Sabei, Bahai, Kakai, and other backgrounds in Iraq, works on championing the idea and practice of "inclusive citizenship."

Peace

Alongside local, informal, and artistic engagement among Christian and Muslim citizens in Egypt, peace is served also by more structured or formal dialogue. *Formal dialogue* is the organized dialogue between leaders of institutions in Egypt. It seeks to establish good communication between institutional representatives of religious organizations. Formal dialogue allows leaders to correct and guide the wrong understandings of religions especially in relation to violence. We have already seen this in the dialogue set up between al-Azhar al-Sharif and the Anglican Communion. The 2002 statement identified the common commitment many Christians and Muslims share to work against religious indifference and religious fanaticism. Such work done by believers might "contribute to international efforts to achieve justice, peace and the welfare of all humanity."[13] The al-Azhar al-Sharif agreement set in motion a series of scholarly exchanges.[14] For example, at the 2004 Anglican–al-Azhar al-Sharif meeting, scholars presented on a range of topics, including Christianity and the West; the Crusades; Christianity and its understanding of power; Jihad; and women in Islam. Through such scholarly engagement, the participants acknowledged that "Christians and Muslims frequently hold misconceptions about each other's beliefs and practices." In scholarly dialogue they committed themselves to working against inaccurate generalizations and to work toward seriously "counteracting inaccurate presentations" of the two faiths.[15] Between 2004 and 2010, a range of scholarly topics were discussed. The issues included how Christianity relates to the state; Christian minorities in Islamic countries; Muslim minorities in Christian countries; the role of the media in interfaith engagement; freedom of expression; the image of Christ; religious leaders and the promotion of the rights of citizenship; religion in violence; Shari'a; Fatwas; religious harmony; justice and equality; and intercommunal violence.[16]

The al-Azhar al-Sharif dialogues also inspired local initiatives in Egypt aimed at developing religious leaders with the capacities for deeper dialogue, leading to greater understanding between the two faiths.[17] Of particular

---

13. "Archbishop to Sign Anglican-Muslim Agreement."
14. "Muslim—al Azhar," Anglican Communion, accessed May 22, 2019, https://www.anglicancommunion.org/inter-religious/muslim.aspx.
15. "Al Azhar Cairo 2004," Anglican Communion, accessed May 22, 2019, https://www.anglicancommunion.org/media/111741/Al-Azhar-Cairo-2004.pdf.
16. "Al Azhar London 2005," Anglican Communion, https://www.anglicancommunion.org/media/111744/Al-Azhar-London-2005.pdf; "Al Azhar Cairo 2006," Anglican Communion, https://www.anglicancommunion.org/media/111747/Al-Azhar-Cairo-2006.pdf; "Al Azhar London 2007," Anglican Communion, https://www.anglicancommunion.org/media/111750/Al-Azhar-London-2007.pdf; "Al Azhar Cairo 2008," Anglican Communion, https://www.anglicancommunion.org/media/111753/Al-Azhar-Cairo-2008.pdf; "Al Azhar Cairo 2010," Anglican Communion, https://www.anglicancommunion.org/media/111756/Al-Azhar-Cairo-2010.pdf. All websites accessed May 22, 2019.
17. "Muslim—al Azhar."

significance in the Egyptian context was the "Imam-Priest Exchange." This interfaith initiative, started in 2013, brought together Muslim and Christian religious leaders. The aims of the program include building lasting friendships with religious leaders across the communities; deepening knowledge about theological commonalities and differences; combating negative stereotypes of Christians and Muslims; further developing interfaith cooperation; and sharing knowledge and expertise for the sake of peace in local communities.[18]

The work of Adyan also began in one specific context: Lebanon. It has now grown to have national, regional, and international impact. One of the most important initiatives that Adyan undertakes toward peace is its "Public Reform Process on Education in Inclusive Citizenship" and its training on "Inclusive Citizenship in the Arab World." The teaching on "inclusive citizenship" began for Adyan with nonformal programs delivered through youth clubs in Lebanon. This program educates 1,000 young girls and boys (15–18 years old) from different backgrounds and regions in Lebanon every year. Adyan has trained 173 educators in 65 partner institutions. In recognition of its impact, in 2013 the program was awarded second place in the UN Alliance of Civilization's international prize for "Living Together Peacefully in a Diverse World." Now, because of a partnership with the Lebanese Ministry of Education and Higher Education (MEHE) and the Center for Educational Research and Development (CERD), it is part of the national curriculum.

Adyan developed and activated the mandatory community service component in high schools, engaging 27,500 students and 1,108 different projects. This equated to 550,000 hours of community service across all of Lebanon. Highlighting public values from a faith-based perspective, the foundation also works for the promotion of values and practices of inclusive citizenship through interfaith collaboration. Through the establishment of a network of experts in charge of religious education in the national religious

18. See the Episcopal/Anglican Diocese of Egypt with North Africa and the Horn of Africa, "Together for a New Egypt: The Imam-Priest Exchange," First Year Report, 2013, accessed October 29, 2019, https://www.ecumenism.net/archive/2013_egypt _report_on_the_imam_priest_exchange.pdf.

institutions and the development of toolkits for Christian and Muslim education, Adyan's resources combine a vision for citizenship based on fundamental public values with a worldview rooted in faith.

Generosity

The Church is visible as a human fellowship through its work in the community, through its preaching and teaching, its prayers and hymns, its confession
and faith, its generous works of mercy and reconciliation. The Church is visible
in the world and its witness is made visible through a ministry of generosity.
Christian spirituality cannot be separated from involvement in the physical
world. In the early Church, love for the poor was an important theme in the
writings of the fathers of the church, and the service included exiles, widows,
orphans, and the sick (Rom. 15:25–29; 2 Cor. 8:9–14; Gal. 2:10). The poor are
the marginalized. They are those distant from the center of society and distant
from the centers of power. Marginality touches all spheres of life and is often so
extensive that people feel they have no resources to do anything about it.

In light of a generous God, the prophetic commitment is justice for the
poor, widows, orphans, strangers, and oppressed (James 1:27). The Bible
emphasizes the reality of human interdependence and the equal dignity and
worth of human beings (Gen. 1:27). Service is at the heart of *koinonia*. The
understanding of the Church as a visible sign is very appropriate to the mission
of the Church in Egypt as a servant. Service is the practical expression of the
life-transforming generous gospel. Christians serve others as Christ, servant of
all, served those who came to him. Faith without works is dead (James 2:26).
Faith, we might also say, without generosity is dead. Indeed, Temple Gairdner
argued that Christians should leave Islam alone unless it could offer a nobler
and higher level of fraternity in practice and not just in rhetoric.[19] For such reasons, Anglicans in Egypt offer social work to Christians and Muslims alike. The
Anglican Church in Egypt serves all Christians and Muslims through its social
centers, hospitals, and schools. Designated centers for special needs and the deaf

---

19. Michael T. Shelley, "Temple Gairdner of Cairo Revisited," *Islam and Christian-
Muslim Relations* 10, no. 3 (1999): 261–78.

are recognized centers of excellence in service to the whole community. Ministry to refugees is also important in an expression of generosity through welcome and through church clinics, schools, and nurseries. In times of crisis, such social work embodies the good intentions of Christians toward their neighbors.

Like the Anglican Church in Egypt, Adyan is convinced that people who abide in spiritual solidarity are those who carry within them all other communities. Adyan is mindful of celebrating the other as the voice of God or the voice of the indescribable in our lives. For Adyan, generosity means hospitality. Based on a two-year research project on dialogue led by two theologians (one Muslim and one Christian), a book entitled *Divine Hospitality: Theology of the Other in Christianity and Islam* was published by Adyan in Arabic (2011) and French (2013) and later in German and English in 2016 and 2017.[20] In the book, Tabbara argues that when the Qur'ān is read chronologically, and not sequentially, three phases can be seen in relation to the "other." The Qur'ān first reminds Muslims that their religion is closely connected to the religions of the "people of the book," with belief in the same God, belief in the same line of prophets, and a call for the same values such as solidarity, generosity, and justice. Second, the Qur'ān directly addresses historical schism and conflict between Muslims and "people of the book." These are the verses that speak about violence and wars between Muslims and "people of the book." Third, following the conflict, the Qur'ān calls for reconciliation and openness to diversity, and celebrates a "fellowship" and "communion" in works done for God despite the irreducible nature of differences across religious communities. It is as if the appeal is for us to see, finally, that "there is *ghayb* (mystery) in the divergence."[21] The final word of the Qur'ān concerning diversity is a call for accepting it as the will of God. We are called, then, to make the best of it in this world through an effort to know each other, to cultivate convivial relations with each other, and to strive together for the common good.

---

20. Fadi Daou and Nayla Tabbara, *Divine Hospitality: A Christian-Muslim Conversation* (Geneva: World Council of Churches, 2017).
21. Daou and Tabbara, *Divine Hospitality*, 101.

Questions for Reflection

8. In your context, where have you seen interreligious friendship, peacebuilding, and generosity?

9. What are the challenges, in your context, to interreligious friendship, peace building, and generosity?

10. What examples in this chapter inspire you to think and act generously toward others different from yourself?

11. Spend some time praying for the leaders of your community, particularly that they would strive for friendship with all, work for peace, and be generous.

Take some time individually or as a group and ask God to help you see new opportunities for generosity, peace, and friendship. After a period of silence, read Philippians 4:4–9 and *Al 'Asr* 103:1–3. Again, sit in silence as you ask God to speak to you about God's generosity, peace, and friendship. Then pray this prayer aloud:

> Lord,
> Allow us to be true witnesses for equity and justice.
> May we never act to gain notoriety
> but act always out of empathy and for healing
> not expecting anything in return, save more justice in this world.
> Forbid us from competing against each other
> Except in our desire to outdo one another in doing good for all.
> May we not know solidarity with our own flock alone
> but be in solidarity with all who suffer—
> whatever their religion, culture, or ethnicity.
> Loving and Generous God,
> we rejoice in your grace and mercy.
> Guide us to those things that are honorable, pure, and pleasing
>   in your sight:
> that we might be a blessing to the world.
> Amin/Amen.

Conclusion

Robert S. Heaney, John Kafwanka K, and Hilda Kabia

> *Prepare your minds for action; discipline yourselves; set all your hope*
> *on the grace that Jesus Christ will bring you when he is revealed.*
> (1 Pet. 1:13)

Witness

This book begins with an emphasis on mission as God's own *witness* to God's self. This is echoed throughout the book as author after author invite us, in the Spirit, to look for and discern the witness of God in the pages of scripture and in each other. This emphasis on the work or agency of God puts in its proper place the work of human witness. We are always dependent upon the Spirit, who is sovereign (John 3:8). Price and Kaoma, in chapter five, demonstrate some practical implications of this. No one culture and no one language fully expresses the richness of God's good news in Christ. That means intercultural partnership is essential for a fuller view of Christ and the gospel. This fuller view and call of God to deeper unity in ecumenical initiatives and progress is increasingly framed in missional terms. It is the one God that calls all God's people to witness to God's love in the world. Giving primacy to such a call to mission, as Burghardt and Gibaut in chapter seven indicate, is the case in ecumenical dialogues, reframes and reinvigorates the possibilities of *walking* together in ecumenical endeavors. Given this, readers will need to reflect on how, in their own contexts, this missional emphasis changes the relationship between churches and religions. In chapter eight,

Amos (a Christian) and Sperber (a Jew) provide one answer to such a question via a reflection on the sacredness of place. Amos submits that the dominant understanding of mission among Anglicans is "presence." Inherent in that understanding of witness is an open heart that listens to others and in doing so listens for the Spirit of God at work in God's world.

Questions for Reflection

1. What chapter in the book most enriched or challenged your understanding of Christian witness in today's world?
2. To what extent do you believe that deeper intercultural understanding and experience will open up fresh visions of the gospel? Have you experienced this already? What might your community do to encourage greater intercultural experience and discernment?
3. What do you understand by the Anglican emphasis on mission as "presence"? What are the opportunities and challenges of this form of witness in your context?

Listening

Listening to others is a second important theme in this book. Beginning with Yarborough and Chery (chapter two)—but also in Hills and Snyman (chapter three), Mapangdol and Ueti (chapter four), and Eaton and Stambaugh (chapter six)—time and again we are invited to see the importance of listening across cultural differences. We are invited to see the importance of listening in disagreement and of being hosts and guests with hearts open to hear and see the risen Christ that we might experience and witness to a deeper sense of mutuality. Without deeper listening, we will make easy and overly simplistic assumptions (chapter two) that leave us open to greater division and schism.

Hills and Snyman (chapter three) lay out some practical examples and practical processes through which we might enter more deeply into understanding and more deeply into disagreement. Disagreement is not, then, treated as a sign of dysfunction but as a sign of ongoing discernment in the gospel. Both chapter three and chapter four provide readings of the road to Emmaus, and it is Mapangdol and Ueti who particularly focus on the necessity of hospitality even amid uncertainty. For Eaton and Stambaugh, hospitality in sharing meals is an important and practical expression of mutuality. They are not blind to the deep sin in church history but are, nonetheless, insistent on calling us to mutuality. Breaking bread together is an act that opens up to us the deeper truths of an interwoven creation. It opens up the call of God to the "beauty way" even when the way is often strewn with ugliness.

Questions for Reflection

4. Can you think of an experience where you or your community felt listened to in deep and meaningful ways? If you can, how has that experience shaped the way you listen to others? If you cannot think of such an experience, what do you think makes for deep listening?

5. To what extent do you think deep listening and listening in disagreement are characteristic of Anglicanism today? How might the Anglican Communion facilitate better listening in agreement and disagreement?

6. What are the fruits of deep listening that you pray for? How will you pray for the Anglican Communion today?

Walking

In several chapters the theme of "walking" and "walking together" is implied or dealt with directly. It is noteworthy that the Emmaus road text (Luke 24:13–35) is interpreted in both chapters three and four in the context of disagreeing well and in the context of hospitality. Mosher and Ahmad (chapter nine) and Shehata and Tabbara (chapter ten) remind us powerfully that in our *walking* as Christians we always walk among believers from other traditions and faiths. It is particularly the relationship between Christianity and Islam that continues to define an acute and important interface for Anglicans today. Both chapters nine and ten begin to explore ways in which Anglicans must not only walk among Muslims but walk *with* them.

It is particularly Mosher and Ahmad who challenge some of the limitations of earlier chapters, urging Anglicans to theologize with interreligious plurality at the foreground and not as the background. Anglicans at local, regional, and international gatherings (including Lambeth Conferences) would do well to be hospitable to the insights and voice of peoples of other faiths as, indeed, this volume has sought to be. For Anglicans, the gains of interreligious dialogue, as well as ecumenical dialogue, can be instructive. Not least among these lessons are the very definitions and practices that emerge and define the task of dialogue. Mosher and Ahmad remind us that dialogue is not debate and "its purpose is the gaining of clarity rather than the winning of an argument. *Dialogue* is a technical term for *transformative activity*—a constellation of strategies employed for the purpose of strengthening relationships or solving problems."

Shehata writes as an Anglican bishop in a Muslim-dominated context. His testimony is to a vibrant and hopeful witness alongside and with Muslims in common commitments in the midst of robust respect for unique claims across religious identities. Tabbara, writing as a Muslim from Lebanon, describes the rich vision and practice of a foundation that sprang from interreligious friendship and is, today, promoting deep listening toward societies that can genuinely serve the common good. Here are leaders involved in promoting principles of walking together in practice and in contexts that have witnessed deep division and violence. With them we pray:

> May we not know solidarity with our own flock alone
> but be in solidarity with all who suffer—
> whatever their religion, culture, or ethnicity.
> Loving and Generous God,
> we rejoice in your grace and mercy.
> Guide us to those things that are honorable, pure, and pleasing
>   in your sight:
> that we might be a blessing to the world.

God's Church for God's World: Witnessing, Listening, Walking

Questions for Reflection

7. *Witnessing:* as you look back on your reading of this book, where did you hear the Spirit particularly witness to you? What is it you have discerned the Spirit say to you in this book? Share this with someone this week.

8. *Listening:* as you listened to the voices in this book, what questions are you left with? How might you resource these questions or get answers to them?

9. *Walking:* to what extent has your thinking been changed or enriched in reading this book? What are you now praying for that you were not praying for before? How will you "walk differently" because of reading this book (that is to say, what will you do differently)?

Three overarching themes emerge from the diversity of authors and chapters in this book. First, there is an emphasis in these pages on the *witness* of God. Our witness is a response to that divine witness and even participation in that divine witness. Second, because it is God who speaks first, our very being emerges from a *listening* soil and listening earth. In Genesis 1 we read, "The Lord God fashioned the human, humus from the soil, and blew into his nostrils the breath of life, and the human became a living creature" (Gen. 2:7).[22] We are alive because we felt the breath of God and heard the word of God (Gen. 1:26; 2:7; John 1:1–5). We witness to the gospel of Christ because we heard the word of God (Heb. 1:1–4). Listening is, then, the first mark of the human being and of gospel ministry. Third, we seek to *walk together* as God's creatures, as believers, and as Anglicans because it is God's will (John 17:22–23). Christians believe that from the one sinful humanity God is creating a renewed and renewing humanity. When Christians strive for, embody,

---

22. *The Hebrew Bible: Volume 1: The Five Books of Moses,* trans. Robert Alter (New York: W.W. Norton & Company, 2019), 14.

and enact greater degrees of walking together, we witness to the truth of God's gospel.

Before you close this book, give thanks to God for such eternal grace. Give thanks to God for the witness of divine love in Jesus. Ask God, in the power of the Spirit, to give you deeper capacity and skills to listen to others and especially to those you disagree with. Pray that God's will for a united church and a redeemed humanity can be honored by your service and ministry in your context.

A Closing Prayer

> God and Father of our Lord Jesus Christ,
> by your great mercy you have given us new birth into a living hope
> through the resurrection of Jesus from the dead.
> Grant us, and those whom we love,
> a deeper sense of your presence
> and a clear vision of your call upon our lives.
> Open our hearts and unstop our ears
> that we might know you in the stranger,
> in the guest, and as the host
> so that, fed by you, we might rise from your table
> to work for the peace and blessing of the world.
> Amen.

Bibliography

Adams, David Foster. *Education for Extinction: American Indians and the Boarding School Experience, 1875–1928*. Lawrence: University Press of Kansas, 1995.

Alter, Robert, trans. *The Hebrew Bible: Volume 1: The Five Books of Moses*. New York: W.W. Norton & Company, 2019.

Anglican Communion. "An Agreement for Dialogue Between the Anglican Communion and al-Azhar al-Sharif." February 2, 2002. https://www .anglicancommunion.org/media/111577/An-agreement-for-dialogue -between-the-Anglican-Communion-and-al-Azhar-al-Sharif.pdf

———. "Generous Love: The Truth of the Gospel and the Call to Dialogue." Accessed August 15, 2019. https://nifcon.anglicancommunion.org /media/18910/generous_love_a4_with_foreward.pdf

———. "Jewish-Anglican Jewish Commission." Accessed August 15, 2019. https://www.anglicancommunion.org/inter-religious/jewish.aspx

———. "Marks of Mission." Accessed March 29, 2019. https://www .anglicancommunion.org/mission/marks-of-mission.aspx

Anglican Congress and Eugene Fairweather. *Anglican Congress 1963: Report of the Proceedings*. Toronto: Editorial Committee Anglican Congress, 1963.

Anglican Consultative Council (2016). Resolution 16.01. Accessed August 20, 2019. https://www.anglicancommunion.org/structures/instruments -of-communion/acc.aspx

Anglican Consultative Council and the Anglican Communion Environmental Network. "The World Is Our Host: A Call to Urgent Action for Climate

Justice." Good Friday 2015. https://acen.anglicancommunion.org/media/148818/The-World-is-our-Host-FINAL-TEXT.pdf

Anglican-Lutheran European Regional Commission. *Anglican-Lutheran Dialogue: The Report of the Anglican-Lutheran European Regional Commission, Helsinki, August–September 1982.* London: SPCK, 1983.

Anglican-Oriental Orthodox International Commission. *Christology: Agreed Statement.* Cairo, 2014. https://www.anglicancommunion.org/media/103502/anglican-oriental-orthodox-agreed-statement-on-christology-cairo-2014.pdf

———. *The Procession and Work of the Holy Spirit: Agreed Statement.* Dublin, 2017. https://www.anglicancommunion.org/media/312561/the-procession-and-work-of-the-holy-spirit-dublin-agreed-statement.pdf

Avis, Paul D.L. *A Ministry Shaped by Mission.* New York: T&T Clark International, 2005.

Badriaki, Michael Bamwesigye. *When Helping Works: Alleviating Fear and Pain in Global Missions.* Eugene, OR: Wipf and Stock, 2017.

Barnes, Jonathan. *Power and Partnership: A History of the Protestant Mission Movement.* Eugene, OR: Pickwick, 2013.

Barrows, John Henry. *The World's Parliament of Religions: An Illustrated and Popular Story of the World's First Parliament of Religions, Held in Chicago in Connection with the Columbian Exposition of 1893.* Vol. 1. Charleston, SC: Nabu Press, 2010.

Battle, Michael. *Reconciliation: The Ubuntu Theology of Desmond Tutu.* Cleveland: Pilgrim Press, 1997.

Benedict of Nursia. *The Holy Rule of St. Benedict.* Translated by Boniface Verheyen (Grand Rapids, MI: Christian Classics Ethereal Library, 1949), chapter LIII, http://www.documentacatholicaomnia.eu/03d/0480-0547,_Benedictus_Nursinus,_Regola,_EN.pdf

Bouyerdene, Ahmed. *Emir Abd el-Kader: Hero and Saint of Islam.* Translated by Gustavo Polit. Bloomington, IN: World Wisdom, 2012.

Breidenthal, Thomas E. *Christian Households: The Sanctification of Nearness.* Cambridge, MA: Cowley Publications, 1997.

The Church: Towards a Common Vision §1, *Faith and Order Paper No. 214.*
Geneva: WCC, 2013.

Correll, J. Lee. *Through White Men's Eyes: A Contribution to Navajo History.*
Window Rock, AZ: Navajo Times Publishing Company, 1976.

Daou, Fadi and Nayla Tabbara. *Divine Hospitality: A Christian-Muslim
Conversation.* Geneva: World Council of Churches, 2017.

de Gruchy, John W. *Reconciliation: Restoring Justice.* London: SCM Press,
2002.

The Episcopal Church. "Christ and People of Other Faiths (1988)." Accessed
August 20, 2019. https://episcopalchurch.org/library/document/christ-and
-people-other-faiths-1988

———. "A Collect for Fridays." In *The Book of Common Prayer and the
Administration of the Sacraments and Other Rites and Ceremonies of the
Church.* New York: Church Publishing Incorporated, 1979. https://
www.episcopalchurch.org/files/book_of_common_prayer.pdf.

Gomaa, Sheikh Ali. "Building Bridges of Understanding." November 17,
2006. *Cambridge Interfaith Programme.* https://www.interfaith.cam.ac.uk
/resources/lecturespapersandspeeches/buildingbridgesofunderstanding

Igreja Episcopal Anglicana do Brasil. *Livro de Oração Comum. (Book of
Common Prayer of the Anglican Episcopal Church of Brazil).* 9ª Edição.
Porto Alegre: Livraria Anglicana, 2009.

Inter-Anglican Theological and Doctrinal Commission. *Communion, Conflict
and Hope: The Kuala Lumpur Report of the Third Inter-Anglican Theological
and Doctrinal Commission.* London: Anglican Communion Office, 2008.

Ipgrave, Michael. "One, Living, Reasonable: The God of Christianity and
Islam." *Journal of Shi'a Islamic Studies* 1, no. 3 (2008): 19–32.

Ipgrave, Michael, and Guy Wilkinson, eds. "Encouraging Reading: Ten Old
Testament Bible Studies for Presence and Engagement." Church of England.
https://www.churchofengland.org/sites/default/files/2019-05/Encouraging
_Reading.pdf

The Journal of Scriptural Reasoning Forum. "What Is SR?" Accessed January
27, 2013. http://jsrforum.lib.virginia.edu/writings/OchFeat.html

Just, Arthur. *An Ongoing Feast.* Collegeville, MN: Liturgical Press, 1993.

Kafwanka, John, and Mark Oxbrow, eds. *Intentional Discipleship and Disciple-Making: An Anglican Guide for Christian Life and Formation.* London: Anglican Consultative Council, 2016.

Kaoma, Kapya J. *Creation Care in Christian Mission.* Oxford: Regnum Studies in Mission, 2016.

Karris, Robert J. *Eating Your Way Through Luke's Gospel.* Collegeville, MN: Liturgical Press, 2006.

Khalidi, Tarif, ed. and trans. *The Muslim Jesus: Sayings and Stories in Islamic Literature.* Cambridge, MA: Harvard University Press, 2001.

Koenig, John. *New Testament Hospitality.* Philadelphia, PA: Fortress Press, 1985.

Lochhead, David. *The Dialogical Imperative: A Christian Reflection on Interfaith Encounter.* Maryknoll, NY: Orbis, 1988.

The Lutheran World Federation. *Mission in Context: Transformation. Reconciliation. Empowerment.* Edited by Jack Messenger. Geneva, Switzerland: Lutheran World Federation Department for Mission and Development, 2004.

———. *The Self-Understanding of the Lutheran Communion: A Study Document.* Edited by the Department of Theology and Public Witness. Geneva: LWF, 2015.

LWF. *The Diaconate as Ecumenical Opportunity: The Hannover Report of the Anglican-Lutheran International Commission,* in *Anglican-Lutheran Agreements, Regional and International 1972–2002.* Geneva: LWF, 2004.

MacDonald, G. Jeffrey. "A Shocking History." *The Living Church,* February 28, 2018. https://livingchurch.org/2018/02/28/a-shocking-history/

Makgoba, Thabo. Foreword to *Creation Care in Christian Mission.* Edited by Kapya J. Kaoma. Oxford: Regnum Studies in Mission, 2016.

Malimela, Langelihle Phakama. "Analyzing Thabo Mbeki's Policy of 'Quiet Diplomacy' in the Zimbabwean Crisis." Master's thesis. University of Cape Town, 2010.

Mbeki, Thabo. "The African Renaissance, South Africa and the World," United Nations University. April 9, 1998. http://www.unu.edu/unupress /mbeki.html

McFague, Sallie. *Life Abundant: Rethinking Theology and Economy for a Planet in Peril.* Minneapolis, MN: Fortress Press, 2007.

Morgenstern, Matthias. "The Deconstruction of the *Adam and Eve* Narrative in Bereshit Rabbah: Variations on the Significance of the Name 'Adam,' the *Image of God* and the Fall and Redemption of Man(kind) in Jewish Late Antiquity." In *New Approaches to Human Dignity in the Context of Qur'ānic Anthropology: The Quest for Humanity.* Edited by Rüdiger Braun and Hüseyin I. Çiçek. Newcastle upon Tyne: Cambridge Scholars, 2017.

Nasr, Seyyed Hossein et al., eds. *The Study Quran: A New Translation and Commentary.* New York: HarperOne, 2015.

Oppegaard, Sven and Gregory Cameron, eds. *Anglican-Lutheran Agreements 1972–2002.* Geneva: LWF, 2004.

Park, Richard S. *Constructing Civility: The Human Good in Christian and Islamic Political Theologies.* Notre Dame: University of Notre Dame Press, 2017.

Pohl, Christine D. "The Healthy Church: Embodying Hospitality." *Catalyst*, February 1, 2003, https://www.catalystresources.org/the-healthy-church -embodying-hospitality/

Pratt, Douglas. "From Edinburgh to Georgetown: Anglican Interfaith Bridge-Building." *Anglican Theological Review* 96, no. 1 (2014): 15–37.

Samkange, Stanlake J.T., and Tommie M. Samkange. *Hunhuism or Ubuntuism: A Zimbabwe Indigenous Political Philosophy.* Salisbury, Rhodesia: Graham Pub., 1980.

Shelley, Michael T. "Temple Gairdner of Cairo Revisited." *Islam and Christian-Muslim Relations* 10, no. 3 (1999): 261–78.

The Standing Commission for Mission of the Anglican Communion. "Establishment of MISSIO." Accessed August 12, 2019. https://www .anglicancommunion.org/media/108016/MISSIO-The-Standing -Commission-for-Mission-of-the-Anglican-Communion.pdf

Stendahl, Krister. "Why I Love the Bible: Beyond Distinctions of Intellect and Spirit, an Ever-Transforming Affair of the Heart." *Harvard Divinity Bulletin* 35, no. 1 (Winter 2007). https://bulletin.hds.harvard.edu/articles/winter2007/why-i-love-bible

Temple, William. *Christianity and Social Order.* New York: Penguin Books, 1942.

Thistlethwaite, Susan Brooks, ed. *Interfaith Just Peacemaking: Jewish, Christian, and Muslim Perspectives on the New Paradigm of Peace and War.* New York: Palgrave Macmillan, 2011.

To Love and Serve the Lord: Diakonia *in the Life of the Church.* The Jerusalem Report of the Anglican-Lutheran International Commission (ALIC III). Geneva: Lutheran World Federation, 2012.

Tutu, Desmond. *An African Prayer Book.* New York: Doubleday, 1995.

———. *God Has a Dream: A Vision of Hope for Our Time.* New York: Doubleday, 2004.

———. *No Future Without Forgiveness.* New York: Doubleday, 1999.

Walls, Andrew and Cathy Ross, eds. *Mission in the 21st Century: Exploring the Five Marks of Global Mission.* Maryknoll, NY: Orbis, 2008.

WCC. "The Community of the Cross of Nails." Coventry Cathedral. Accessed August 13, 2019. http://www.coventrycathedral.org.uk/ccn/about-us-2/

Williams, Rowan. Foreword to *Mission in the 21st Century: Exploring the Five Marks of Global Mission.* Edited by Andrew Walls and Cathy Ross. Maryknoll, NY: Orbis, 2008.

———. *Meeting God in Paul: Reflections for the Season of Lent.* London: SPCK Publishing, 2015.

Wright, Tom. *Paul: A Biography.* London: SPCK Publishing, 2018.

Yankelovich, Daniel. *The Magic of Dialogue: Transforming Conflict into Cooperation.* New York: Touchstone, 1999.

Additional Resources

Avis, Paul. *The Vocation of Anglicanism*. London: Bloomsbury T&T Clark, 2016.

Chapman, Mark D. *Anglicanism: A Very Short Introduction*. Oxford: Oxford University Press, 2006.

Chapman, Mark D., Sathianathan Clarke, and Martyn Percy, eds. *The Oxford Handbook of Anglican Studies*. Oxford: Oxford University Press, 2016.

Douglas, Ian T. and Pui-lan Kwok. *Beyond Colonial Anglicanism: The Anglican Communion in the Twenty-First Century*. New York: Church Publishing, 2001.

Goodhew, David, ed. *Growth and Decline in the Anglican Communion: 1980 to the Present*. Routledge Contemporary Ecclesiology. London: Routledge, 2017.

Hanciles, Jehu. *Beyond Christendom: Globalization, African Migration, and the Transformation of the West*. Maryknoll, NY: Orbis Press, 2008.

Heaney, Robert S. and William Sachs. *The Promise of Anglicanism*. London: SCM Press, 2019.

Inter-Anglican Standing Commission on Unity, Faith & Order. *Towards a Symphony of Instruments: A Historical and Theological Consideration of the Instruments of Communion of the Anglican Communion*. London: Anglican Consultative Council, 2018.

Jarra, C. "Dialogue for Peaceful Co-Existence between Christians and Muslims: The Sociological Dimension." In *From the Cross to the Crescent*, edited by J.A. Mbillah and J. Chesworth, 86–97. Nairobi: Procmura, 2004.

Katongole, Emmanuel. *Born from Lament: The Theology and Politics of Hope in Africa*. Grand Rapids, MI: Eerdmans, 2017.

Keller, Catherine, Michael Nausner, and Mayra Rivera, eds. *Postcolonial Theologies: Divinity and Empire*. St. Louis, MO: Chalice Press, 2004.

Kwok, Pui-lan, ed. *Anglican Women on Church and Mission*. Canterbury Studies in Anglicanism. Harrisburg, PA: Morehouse, 2012.

Lambeth Conference 2020. https://www.lambethconference.org/

McGrath, Alister E. *The Renewal of Anglicanism*. Harrisburg, PA: Morehouse, 1993.

Mugambi, J.N.K. *Christian Theology and Social Reconstruction*. Nairobi: Acton, 2003.

Omari, C.K. *What Christians Should Know about Islam*. Nairobi: Pauline Publications Africa, 2003.

Pestana, Carla Gardina. *Protestant Empire: Religion and the Making of the British Atlantic World*. Philadelphia: University of Pennsylvania Press, 2009.

Sachs, William L. *The Oxford History of Anglicanism: Global Anglicanism, c. 1910–2000*. Vol. V. Oxford: Oxford University Press, 2018.

Sanneh, Lamin. *Translating the Message: The Missionary Impact on Culture*. Maryknoll, NY: Orbis Press, 2009 [1989].

Swamy, Muthuraj. *Walking Together: Global Anglican Perspectives on Reconciliation*. Kindle Edition. Amazon Digital Services, 2019.

————. *Witnessing Together: Global Anglican Perspectives on Evangelism and Witness*. Kindle Edition. Amazon Digital Services, 2019.

Thomas, M. *What Muslims Should Know about Christianity*. Nairobi: Pauline Publications Africa, 2002.

Wafula, R.S., Esther Mombo, and Joseph Wandera, eds. *The Postcolonial Church: Bible, Theology, and Mission*. Alameda, CA: Borderless Press, 2016.

Ward, Kevin. *A History of Global Anglicanism*. New York: Cambridge University Press, 2006.

Wells, Samuel. *What Anglicans Believe: An Introduction*. Harrisburg, PA: Morehouse, 2011.

Wijsen, F., and B. Mfumbusa. *Seeds of Conflict*. Nairobi: Pauline Publications Africa, 2002.

Woodley, Randy S. *Shalom and the Community of Creation: An Indigenous Vision*. Grand Rapids, MI: Eerdmans, 2012.

About the Authors

Najah Nadi Ahmad has worked as a contributing editor for the Integrated Encyclopaedia of the Qur'ān, and has taught in Egypt, the UK, and the USA. She is fellow in peace and reconciliation at Virginia Theological Seminary's Center for Anglican Communion Studies and a junior fellow at the Holberg Seminar on Islamic History at Princeton University.

Clare Amos prior to retirement headed the office of Interreligious Dialogue and Cooperation at the World Council of Churches, and served as the director of theological studies in the Anglican Communion Office. Still actively involved with theological, biblical, ecumenical, and interreligious initiatives, she is currently working on a book exploring the "transfiguration" in Christian theology.

Anne Burghardt, a Lutheran pastor, has worked in the Department of Public Theology and Witness at the Lutheran World Federation and as an editor on a number of recently published works. She has been cosecretary of the Anglican-Lutheran International Coordinating Committee and is currently a member of the Lutheran-Orthodox / Lutheran-Pentecostal dialogues, and the governing board of the Conference of European Churches.

Marie Carmel Chery, a theologian from Haiti, is a librarian and storyteller who became the second female ordained minister of the Episcopal Church of Haiti in 2012. She is priest-in-charge of two churches and two schools, Epiphany and Good Shepherd.

Cornelia Eaton serves as the canon to the ordinary for ministry of the Episcopal Church in Navajoland. She serves on the Executive Council of the Episcopal Church. She is a member of the Salt Clan people of the *Diné* (Navajo). Her faith and practice is rooted in the Navajo ancestral perspective and the theology and traditions of the Anglican Communion.

John Gibaut is currently president of Thorneloe University, Sudbury, Canada. From 2015, he served as the director for unity, faith, and order at the Anglican Communion Office. From 2008, he was the director of the Commission on Faith and Order at the World Council of Churches.

Robert S. Heaney is associate professor of Christian mission at the Virginia Theological Seminary and also the director of the seminary's Center for Anglican Communion Studies. He is the author of a number of books and articles on Anglican identity, mission, interfaith dialogue, and postcolonial theology. He serves on the Lambeth 2020 Design Group.

Sarah Hills was born in South Africa, brought up in Northern Ireland, and has lived in England since the mid-1980s. A qualified psychiatrist and psychotherapist, she was ordained in 2007 and currently serves as vicar of Holy Island. She is canon emeritus for reconciliation at Coventry Cathedral; canon for reconciliation for the primus of Scotland; visiting fellow at St. John's College, Durham; and visiting practice fellow at Coventry University.

Hilda Kedmond Kabia is the first female principal of Msalato Theological College in Tanzania. She has held positions as chairperson for the House of Clergy; general secretary to the Synod; lecturer; deanery youth secretary and secretary of the Diocese of Central Tanganyika's Women's Department.

John Kafwanka K is the director for mission for the Anglican Communion. He oversees work that promotes mission in the Communion, including the Communion's Intentional Discipleship initiative. Previously he served as principal of the national Theological College of the Anglican Church in Zambia (St John's Seminary), and thereafter as Church Mission Society's regional manager for Southern Africa. John has and continues to serve on a number of ecumenical and international bodies and charities.

John Kapya Kaoma is a Zambian Anglican priest, visiting researcher at Boston University Center for Global Christianity and Mission, and distinguished visiting professor at St. John's University College in Zambia.

Gloria Lita D. Mapangdol is a priest of the Episcopal Church in the Philippines. Since 2014, she has served as the president and dean of Saint Andrew's Theological Seminary—the only Anglican/Episcopalian seminary in the Philippines—where she teaches New Testament.

Lucinda Mosher is fellow in world Anglicanism in Virginia Theological Seminary's Center for Anglican Communion Studies; faculty associate in interfaith studies at Hartford Seminary, and affiliated with its Macdonald Center for the Study of Islam and Christian-Muslim Relations; and assistant academic director of the Building Bridges Seminar, a dialogue of Christian and Muslim scholars.

Janice Price is world mission adviser for the Archbishops' Council of the Church of England. Previously she was director of the Global Mission Network of Churches' Together in Britain and Ireland. She has worked in local churches in rural, suburban, and urban contexts as a licensed lay minister for over thirty years.

Samy Fawzy Shehata was ordained in 1990. He served as an assistant to the bishop and in various leadership positions in Alexandria, Egypt, planning and developing ministry teams. He has also taught at Alexandria School of Theology and was consecrated area bishop for the Episcopal area of North Africa in the Diocese of Egypt in 2017.

Deon Snyman is the chief operating officer of the Restitution Foundation based in Cape Town. He trained as a theologian at the University of Pretoria and previously worked in Zulu-speaking congregations of the Uniting

Reformed Church in Northern Zululand and as priority issues manager of the Diakonia Council of Churches in Durban, South Africa.

Daniel Sperber is the Milan Roven Professor of Talmud at Bar-Ilan University in Israel, and the president of the Ludwig and Erica Jesselson Institute for Advanced Torah Studies. In addition, Rabbi Sperber has been a member of the Anglican-Chief Rabbinate dialogue commission between 2006 and 2018. In 1992, he won the prestigious Israel Prize for his contribution to Jewish cultural life.

James Stambaugh is rector of the Church of the Holy Apostles in Wynnewood, in the Episcopal Diocese of Pennsylvania. He was born in northern New Mexico and grew up in the central Rio Grande Valley. James earned his master of divinity degree at Virginia Theological Seminary in 2017.

Nayla Tabbara is director of the Institute of Citizenship and Diversity Management at Adyan Foundation. A professor in religious and Islamic studies, she has received the Gold Medal of the French Renaissance award and the Special Jury award of the Fr. Jacques Hamel Prize, and the Ecritures et Spiritualités Award for her book *L'islam pensé par une femme*.

Paulo Ueti, Brazilian mestizo (Japanese mom and Italian father) was raised in a multicultural environment. He is a New Testament biblical scholar, working for the Anglican Alliance and Theological Education Department of the Anglican Communion; a professor of biblical hermeneutics at Asian Theologian Academy, Sri Lanka; and a member of the Ecumenical Centre of Biblical Studies Brazil, Brazilian Association for Biblical Research (ABIB), and SBL/USA.

Alan Yarborough currently works in communications for the Episcopal Church Office of Government Relations, and is responsible for the resources aimed at educating, equipping, and engaging the church in policy advocacy. Prior to this, he worked in Haiti as part of the Young Adult Service Corps and as a project manager for agricultural revitalization.

Lightning Source UK Ltd.
Milton Keynes UK
UKHW020641270820
368907UK00006B/250